A Woman of Faith
Evangeline

A Woman *of* Faith
Evangeline

BETTE
NORDBERG

CANNON BEACH
CHRISTIAN CONFERENCE CENTER

Scripture quotations are taken from the King James Version of the Bible.

Evangeline: A Woman of Faith
Copyright ©2005 Bette Nordberg
All rights reserved

Cover Design by Bruce DeRoos of Left Coast Design
Interior Design by Pine Hill Graphics

Packaged by Wordsmith Books, LLC
P.O. Box 68065, Seattle, WA 98168

Library of Congress Cataloging-in-Publication Data
(Provided by Cassidy Cataloguing Services, Inc.)

Nordberg, Bette.

    Evangeline : a woman of faith / Bette Nordberg. -- 1st ed. -- Cannon
Beach, Ore. : Cannon Beach, 2005

       p. ; cm.

      ISBN: 1-933150-08-4
      ISBN-13: 978-1-933150-08-6

    1. McNeill, Evangeline. 2. Cannon Beach Conference Center
(Cannon Beach, Ore.) 3. Christian leadership--Biography.
4. Christian biography. 5. Christian life. 6. Spirituality. I. Title.

BR1725.M366 N67 2005
270/.092--dc22   0507

Printed in the United States of America.

To David Jeremiah, who said,
"Be ready to take the hill country."

To Cheryl, who said,
"You can do it."

And to Jill Jaquard,
who gave me the tools to finish,

Many Thanks.

Preface

*T*his story is largely the result of interviews and information gathered by Joe and Louise Noegel over a five-year period ending in 1990. Each story and the details and conversations included are taken directly from tapes of interviews with those involved. Evangeline was what some would term a pack rat, leaving numerous boxes of personal effects to her daughter Heather. Among these treasures, Evangeline kept sermon notes, conference planning notes, ticket stubs, letters and drafts of her own correspondence. After pouring through this collection, the items were separated into manila envelopes by date. From these envelopes a relatively accurate picture of her activities could be determined. The details were fleshed out by particularly helpful interviews with her brother, Walter Duff.

While memories fade over the years, Evangeline McNeill took the time to write many of these stories during the last years of her life. An excellent writer, her effort to tell the whole story was cut short by her death in 1977. Some liberty has been taken to fill in the emotions and thoughts of the main characters. It is our hope that this story is both accurate and readable, while at the same time compelling and inspiring. Evangeline McNeill certainly displayed all of these qualities.

Contents

Prologue

*I*t is morning at the beach. And as I push away the sleepiness that envelops me, I dress quickly, careful not to wake the children. Sneaking outside, I find the air is clear and fresh, though chilly, even for August. I zip up my jacket and pull the collar around my neck. Though it is foggy, there is a striking brightness to the day. Experience assures me that the sun will burn through before the morning ends.

I reach Whale Park quickly and stop at the end of the path to wonder again at the breathtaking beauty of the beach. Wheat-colored sand spreads out in every direction. Here the beach is both very deep and miles long. A sleepy creek winds its way across the beach toward the ocean, as though in no hurry to lose its identity in the sea. On my right, to the north, a rocky point juts out into the waves. In the distance, even through the fog, I recognize the old lighthouse that holds its usual position on the rocks. I strike out toward the south, wading through the wide span of sand to arrive at the edge of the creek.

From there, I enjoy a comfortable walk on hard sand to "the rock." In Cannon Beach, Oregon, "the rock" refers to Haystack Rock, an enormous basalt sentry standing guard at the southernmost end of the village beach. A sanctuary for nesting birds, it is the largest monolith on the coast of the continental United States. At its base, enormous tide pools host a great variety of coastal sea life. During low tides crowds of families poke and point at protected anemones, starfish and crabs.

On this particular morning, I pause to listen again to the sound of the ocean. It is not the mellow lapping of a pond—or even the crash of singular waves. But rather, I hear the sound of the waves from every direction, melting together in a great symphony of sound, an almost deafening roar at this close range.

For those of us who love this beach, this sound can be called back at any time. It is stored forever, along with the feel of the wind, the sound of the gulls and the smell of the tide. Always in my memory is the unending noise of the ocean.

This memory is so strong that over and over it draws me back to the source, as it has this morning, ever returning to experience the magnificence of the setting. Back again to experience the power of it. Back again to watch the personality of the ocean change with the seasons and the weather.

At 7:30 A.M. I find the beach busy with people. Like ants in their divinely directed path, these visitors move as though on pilgrimage. Beginning at Whale Park on the north end of the village, they, like me, cross the beach and head for "the rock." Some walk alone, others in pairs or groups.

Holding hands as they move briskly down the beach, young couples bow their heads, deep in conversation. Some move more slowly, white "hairdos" protected from beach winds with telltale chiffon scarves. Some are pairs of women. Others are couples long used to pacing each other on their morning trek to the rock. Sometimes a parent accompanies a child or two, with the youngest holding the honored position on top of daddy's shoulders.

An uninformed observer would wonder, as we do with ants, the meaning of the procession. He would ponder the exactness of the path, and its timing. But I have no questions; I know because I share their secret.

The mystery of this place is *our* secret.

We have come not for the majesty of the Pacific Coast of Oregon—though this is majesty enough, but for something more—more magnificent, more powerful.

Cannon Beach Christian Conference Center resides here. For more than sixty years, the conference center has provided valuable family programs—both week-long summer conferences and a full winter schedule of individual and church retreat programs—designed to promote the growth and maturity of the Body of Christ.

For some reason, though none can explain it, there is a hole in the heavens here. And through the hole, the God who created this grandeur pours Himself out to His people. Here, He speaks. Here, He comforts. Here, He heals, restores and refreshes.

The secret lies in the ministry.

This is why all these people, of every age and social circumstance, flock to this place. They come to experience this heavenly outpouring. They come to encounter this comforting, healing, restoring, refreshing Heavenly Father.

The story of this place began years ago—with the story of a couple—a couple devoted to one another, and devoted to their God. It is the story of one woman's conviction and perseverance. Yet more than the story of a place, or a person, it is the story of God working through people.

CHAPTER ONE

Summer's End

Some days seem destined for disaster. The alarm doesn't go off. The bus comes late. You forget your lunch.

But other days give no hint of the tragedy to come.

Tuesday, August 5, 1952 dawned without portent. As the sun rose, the sky along the Oregon coast took on a clear, brilliant blue. By the time breakfast ended, those at Cannon Beach Bible Conference already felt uncomfortably warm. According to the radio, by day's end temperatures in Portland would reach 105 degrees. But the weather forecast did not dampen the enthusiasm of conference guests; they expected ocean breezes to moderate temperatures along the coast. Even as they left the dining hall, guests anticipated a day of outside activities in the extraordinarily perfect weather.

As Evangeline Duff McNeil watched her guests leave the dining hall, she felt satisfied. So far, the week had gone well. While those around her enjoyed the last of the breakfast conversation, she found herself thinking about the conference center's progress. In only seven years, it had grown and matured beyond her expectations. Guests no longer brought ration books with them on vacation. The specter of war did not hover over their conferences. Though it was still only a fledgling operation,

Evangeline and her husband, Archie held so much hope for the future. They had plans for the place—big plans.

Before they bought the property, Archie believed that people from all over the northwest would want to come to the Oregon coast to enjoy the best of the nation's Bible teachers. The restful, recreational setting would allow them to relax and focus on the messages. As she sipped her tea, Evangeline shook her head and smiled.

Archie's prediction proved absolutely correct. Not only had guests chosen to come to the beach, God's abundant blessing seemed to cover the Bible Conference. Over and over, God miraculously provided for the needs of the conference center. Watching Him work gave Evangeline great joy.

The conference center belonged to God. It was His project. And by virtue of their mutual calling it became an obsession for Archie and Evangeline. In prayer and in hard work, they had given birth to it, watched it grow, and guided it toward maturity.

Evangeline watched Archie as he visited with guests. Even after sixteen years, her love for him surprised her. People called Archie a real "platform man." But he was gifted in many ways. Even hosting breakfast is an art form to him, she mused. A giant of a man, six feet four inches, weighing nearly 260 pounds, his rich Scottish brogue and warm friendly manner enabled conference center guests to become a part of a much larger family. Though they arrived as strangers, they left as friends.

Each week, Archie and Evangeline watched rich and lasting relationships develop between guests. Believing in the importance and significance of each guest, they worked together to make all feel welcome—Archie from the platform, and Evangeline in her own personal, almost motherly way.

On this clear, warm morning, with breakfast over, and the guests dismissed, Archie moved quickly toward the table where Evangeline sat with her brother Walter Duff, and his wife, Edith. "I'm headed into Portland now," he said, patting her hand.

"Don't you want me to come along?" she asked.

"No, you stay here. It's too hot for you to sit in the car waiting for me."

As she walked him toward the car she asked again. "Are you sure Archie? I always come along." With a hug and kiss, he insisted she stay behind.

A small village on the North Oregon coast, Cannon Beach offered little in the way of grocery and restaurant supplies. During the summer months, Archie made the weekly trip to Portland himself. As Evangeline watched Archie's car head onto the street, she felt uneasy about not going along. She shook the thought away, and returned to the lodge.

As Evangeline went about her daily tasks, she found herself remembering other trips to Portland. She thought fondly of silent hours in the car holding hands. Were other couples able to spend hours enveloped in the same quiet world of love and understanding? He had always wanted her with him, always enjoyed her company.

Even when he was away for a speaking engagement, invariably Archie called late in the evening saying, "I just arrived in Portland. I'll be home as soon as I can." No matter how late, or how much Evangeline begged for him to spend the night in the city, Archie would head directly for Cannon Beach.

He hated to stay away when he was so close to home.

In those days, the Sunset Highway, which led from Portland to the coast, was carved into the rugged coastal mountains. It was a tortuous drive, even for well-rested drivers in daylight hours. Over the years, she had spent many sleepless hours praying as she waited to hear his car turn on to the gravel driveway of the conference center.

Later that morning, Isabelle, fourteen, asked to take little Helen Jean for a walk to the beach. Evangeline gave her permission, glad to have the children occupied. Isabelle loved caring for Helen Jean. Though they were 10 years apart, they enjoyed one another's company. Evangeline busied herself again with her guests and conference responsibilities trying to shake the uneasy feelings that surrounded her thoughts.

⚜

When Bob and Sally McGrath arrived at the conference center they were tired and hungry. They had survived the long drive from Seattle, Washington, to Cannon Beach, Oregon with two children. Not knowing anything about the center's work, Bob had agreed to lead the worship in exchange for room and board. Though it might not be much of a vacation, it was free. By the time they climbed the stairs of the old log hotel, Bob knew that Sally was disappointed in the arrangement.

The upper floor was dark and unheated, and the walls between the rooms were made of boards riddled with open knotholes. Clouds of smoke filled the upstairs hallway—the only evidence of the working stove downstairs. The vacation might be free, he thought watching Sally's face, but the cost was too high. In spite of his disappointment in the facilities, Bob put his all into the services. As the week progressed, he and Sally found themselves irresistibly drawn to the spirit of the place and the graciousness of their host and hostess.

The smoke in the upstairs hallway had not disappeared, yet somehow, it didn't matter as much.

⚜

The unusual heat of Tuesday, August 5, filled the fire station with the smell of perspiration and the sounds of irritability. Pete, the station commander realized that his crew wished they were somewhere else. Everyone seemed to feel sleepy, moving in slow motion. However, his sluggishness evaporated when he heard the radio call his fire team to an accident on the Sunset highway.

No matter how often he saw them, Pete never viewed the tragedy of a collision lightly. As the accident came into view, a sick, heavy feeling settled in his stomach. A large dump truck lay on its side in the ditch. A late model maroon sedan had come to rest across the highway—its front end nearly nonexistent. Broken glass was everywhere. Pete saw the driver of the car slumped over the steering wheel. Eggshells and flour were strewn all over the hillside.

Pete's crew split up immediately, some to help the driver of the truck, who seemed only slightly injured. Some went immediately to the car. Gently, they lifted the large middle-aged man onto the roadway where the medical team took over. Though the injured man was conscious, Pete's experienced eyes could see that he was badly hurt. Where was the ambulance?

By the time he arrived, onlookers had already gathered. "Like vultures," Pete muttered. Turning his attention to the growing traffic problem, he tried to find a way to move cars around the scene. The truck driver had only scratches, and the State Patrol was busy taking his statement.

The injured man raised his head from the pavement and called loudly, "Does anyone here know how to pray?" Pete felt his queasiness return, and he quickly made his way back to the injured man. As he approached, he heard the man say, "Then I'll pray 'meeself."

Though Pete believed he'd seen it all, he felt his eyes fill with tears as he listened to this man pray. The tenderness of the words were so unlike the cursing that frequented the fire station. As he listened, Pete felt the prayer evoke some new and strange emotion. His sadness deepened as he watched the man's life slip away.

✦

Having finished her accounting at the Cannon Beach Bible Conference, Mrs. Winifred Rupel made her way to the village bus stop. Perspiring heavily, she reached up to tuck a stray piece of white hair back into her chignon, wishing she had not made this commitment.

Winifred had a meeting in Portland, and she settled her grandmotherly bulk onto a bench to wait for the bus. Sitting there in the sun, she was sorry to leave the comfortable breezes of the coast. Surely, she thought, the same sun would make the city heat oppressive. Still, she hoisted herself up the bus steps and settled in for the familiar ride up the Sunset Highway.

Facing a long, slow trip with many stops along the way, Winifred studied the magazine she'd brought along. Not far up the highway, the bus ground to a stop. From the long line of cars ahead, Winifred felt certain they had come upon an accident. Checking her watch, she recalculated the time it would take to reach Portland. She didn't want to see an accident. She hoped they would pass quickly.

Minutes crept by as they made slow progress. Cars filed the other direction in long slow chains. The bus inched forward as they took turns using one lane around the accident. The passengers grew impatient, stirring in their seats, muttering about the delay. As they neared the scene, Winifred glanced up from her magazine and was surprised to see a familiar car. Surely it wasn't Archie's maroon Kaiser!

Then as the bus drew nearer still, her surprise turned to horror as she saw a body lying on the highway. Partially covered, with people standing all around it, she could not be absolutely certain.

"Wait," she called out, moving quickly up the aisle, "You must stop—please—" she implored. "I know that man—please—you must let me off here."

The driver would not stop. Anxious and tearful, Winifred got off the bus at the next village. In desperation and fear, she called the coast.

⁕

Evangeline's brothers rarely managed to stay at the conference center at the same time. It was even more unusual to have her sister from Missouri join them there. As children of immigrant parents, they had always been very close. Walter Duff Jr. directed Village Missions from Dallas, Oregon. Haldane Duff, the youngest child, pastored a church in Seattle, Washington. Helen, the oldest of the Duff children managed Christian Women's Clubs and Councils.

Their many speaking engagements, and the demands of their work kept them from coming to the coast to visit. But this summer was different. By some delightful miracle, they had all come during the same week. Only their youngest sister Olive, who lived with her husband and family in California, had not joined them. Evangeline had been thrilled to have her family join her.

⟨ ～≈≈≈≈≈≈ ⟩

When the conference receptionist brought a phone message to Walter, he was very surprised. *Who would know to contact me here*, he wondered. Excusing himself, he went to the phone booth in the lobby of the old log house to return the call. When he rejoined his wife Edith, and his brother Haldane, he reported what little news he had.

As yet, he was not even sure that it was Archie's little car on the highway. Together they agreed to distract Evangeline as Walter made the necessary calls for more information. While Edith and Haldane blocked the view of the phone booth, Walter called hospitals, county and state police. No one had any information. Disappointed, he waited for a patrol officer to return his call.

When the call finally came, the officer confirmed that Archie had indeed been in a terrible accident. He went on and on about the details of the accident. Impatient, Walter interrupted him, "But what about Archie?"

"Oh," he returned flatly. "He's dead."

⟨ ～≈≈≈≈≈≈ ⟩

Evangeline was surprised that Archie had not returned by dinnertime. Mentally she went over his errand list, calculating how much time each would require. Checking her watch again, she decided she would take his place at the evening prayer meeting. Whatever other prayer requests were made that evening, Evangeline had only one. "Bring Archie home safely Lord," she prayed. Was it her imagination or had her words bounced like echoes from the ceiling of the meeting room?

After prayer, Evangeline greeted her guests. Then she walked outside to discover her entire family, including her in-laws, all gathered near the phone booth of the old log house. Before she could ask, Walter came toward her. Anguish twisted the features of his face.

"Evangeline dear, I want to talk to you," he said. Putting an arm around her, he led her to the little cabin she shared with Archie. As she sat down on their bed, he told her as gently as he could about the car accident.

"You mean he's gone?—He's dead?" Evangeline struggled to understand. Wanting not to believe, and yet seeing the truth in her brother's eyes, she felt tears begin to flow down her cheeks. At last the realization came. She had lost her best friend, her lover, her sweetheart.

Archie had been her pastor, her partner, and her favorite preacher. With his beautiful baritone voice, they had performed together, held meetings together, and prayed together. Together they had given birth to two children. They had laughed together. They had grieved together.

Evangeline meant to share life only with him. How could he leave her? Her sense of purpose was wrapped up in him. In those first few moments of grief, all she felt was emptiness—the deepest, most lonely emptiness she had ever experienced. All she had ever wanted or needed was wrapped up in Archie. How could she go on without him?

Chapter Two

The Darkest Winter

*For Evangeline, the winter of 1952 began on the day Archie died.

Without Archie, even the August heat felt cold and dark. Fortunately, Evangeline's family stayed nearby, eager to help. Her initial shock soon gave way to inconsolable weeping. After nearly two days, her desperate family sought the help of Evangeline's physician. Medication helped her rest for the days and decisions ahead. As Evangeline's mother took over the care of Isabelle and Helen Jean, Evangeline's brothers cared for the conference center guests.

In seclusion, Evangeline relived much of the triumph and grief of their past years together. Since the purchase of the conference center, she and Archie had been together constantly. They had planned, dreamed, and worked together on every aspect of their dream. Together they had scrubbed and cleaned and painted. They had formed a corporation and renamed the historic hotel building. They had prepared the outbuildings to house additional visitors. Together they had waited for the arrival of their first guests in July of 1945.

Surprised by the initial success of the work, they had been even more surprised when the following summer, guests came to Archie saying, "God's hand is on this work. We think you should build a dining hall." They suggested using volunteer labor, inviting men to come to work for an organized "work week." That year they hosted the first of many such weeks. Each spring, men who believed in the ministry had given their time and skills to help the center grow.

For that first project, God brought an engineer and a builder. Even in her grief, Evangeline remembered cooking huge meals for the work crews. How she had looked forward to the arrival and enthusiastic support of the work crews. Archie had always taken pictures of their projects and helped wherever he could. He loved to be part of the action. These memories, precious as they were, brought Evangeline fresh tears.

She remembered the joy of Helen Jean's birth. After Isabelle was born, they had wondered if they would ever have another child. How they had rejoiced to bring their second baby home to Cannon Beach. Nearly four, Helen Jean was far too young to understand what had happened to her daddy. How would Evangeline tell her? How could Evangeline explain what she did not understand herself?

Isabelle adored her father. Archie had a singular connection with her—something special that Evangeline could not recreate. Isabelle and Archie had bonded in a way that mystified Evangeline. For Isabelle, there could be no substitute for Archie.

She had other worries too. How could Evangeline support the girls? How could she provide the stability and encouragement that Archie found so natural? She had no money. They had never taken a salary. Every penny had gone back into expansion of the conference center.

Evangeline's deep grief reduced her faith to simple and frequent cries for help. What would she do? How could she carry on without Archie? What would happen to the work? She saw no easy answers.

Over the next few days, hundreds of letters came to the conference center from all parts of the world. Telegrams arrived every few minutes. The grounds swelled with people who came in response to Archie's death. These included members of their old Portland church, people from the Service Men's Center where Archie had ministered during the war, business and civic leaders from everywhere.

Though she could not meet with all of them, Evangeline sensed their presence, their support, and their prayers. Her sister Olive came from California. Somehow, Evangeline managed to help her family plan two services for Archie, one on the grounds at Cannon Beach, the other at the funeral home in Portland. She managed to record the services so that she could send tapes to Archie's mother in England. Activity became a tonic to her. Slowly she returned to herself.

Though she survived the funeral and burial services, the future looked bleak to Evangeline. Like an anvil, loneliness set in. She longed to care about the work of the conference center. But everything about it reminded her that Archie was gone. She continued to pray. But each day seemed colder, darker, and more lonely than the day before.

After the funeral, Dr. J. Vernon McGee took her aside. "It is a great work you do here, and it must continue," he said. "It is one of the most unique Bible conferences in the entire nation. However, it is clearly not a woman's work." Dr. McGee paused to let the words sink in. "Evangeline, Archie is gone. You must get a man in here to do it."

How could she give away the conference center? It was Archie's—hers—theirs. To give away the leadership would be like abandoning the baby they had conceived together. She could not do it.

From the time she was old enough to understand the gospel, Evangeline's father had trained her for ministry. Evangeline's father saw no difference between men and women in the kingdom of God. If a person could speak, a person could minister the Gospel of Jesus Christ. He felt that all Christians would be needed—male and female—to reach the world for Christ.

Evangeline could not see things any other way. The more she considered it, the more confident she became. Though Archie was gone, Jesus was not. Jesus had given this dream to them. He had brought them this far. He would bring her the rest of the way. Though struggling with sadness and grief, Evangeline would not quit. Taking pencil in hand, she wrote the rough draft of what would become the conference center's fall newsletter:

"I've thought about it so many, many times, in the daytime and at night and in the middle of the night. I know what God would have me do—continue! I know what dear Archie would have me do—continue! The conference board met at the close of the season and agreed we should surely press on in this work, which God has blessed so singularly in these past eight years. Do pray that God will give me the wisdom and strength to carry on this ministry."

<hr>

Evangeline had determined *what* she would do, but the problem of *how* she would do it remained. How could she support herself during the long winter ahead? The cold, rainy Oregon coast was not conducive to winter conferences. Until his death, she and Archie had spent the winter months holding evangelistic meetings for various churches along the west coast. Before Isabelle entered school, she too had traveled with them.

But Evangeline couldn't hold those meetings alone. How could Evangeline support herself, the girls, and the Bible Conference?

Though Evangeline's family encouraged her to carry on the work of the conference, they wondered about her support as well. They had watched as Evangeline and Archie birthed the dream and nurtured it along. They would do whatever was needed to help her bring it to maturity.

The week after Archie's funeral, a summer conference for the Christian Women's Clubs and Councils was scheduled. As Helen supervised the conference, she watched Evangeline with the ladies who had come to the meetings. Suddenly, the answer came to Helen. She wasted no time presenting her idea to the family.

"Evangeline has always been instrumental in starting Women's Clubs and Councils. No one knows how to help those ladies better than Evangeline. Our ministry desperately needs her help. She could come back to Missouri and spend the winter at our headquarters with us. We would be able to pay her a small stipend and send her out speaking and organizing new groups all over the United States. We have more requests for help than we could ever fill on our own. It's the perfect place for Evangeline."

To Evangeline, the suggestion seemed like an answer from heaven. By serving with Christian Women's Clubs and Councils, Evangeline could support her family while at the same time supervising the summer conference schedule. Best of all, in Missouri Evangeline would avoid the loneliness of a dark, wet Oregon winter.

In the spring of 1952 Helen had moved the headquarters of the Christian Business and Professional Women's Council and its co-organization Youth Home Missions to Kansas City, Missouri. After six years in Fort Wayne, Indiana, the need for office and living space had forced them to look for a new and larger location. God had miraculously supplied a seven-and-one-half acre parcel complete with a seventeen-room house, stables and greenhouse.

In 1949, the Women's council had given birth to a new ministry called Village Missions, which supplied small rural communities with qualified pastors. Not long after its inception, Evangeline's brother, Walter Duff Jr., resigned his pastorate in Sunnyside, Washington to supervise the new work. Once again the Duff family was training and sending Christian workers into the world.

Evangeline's mother, Mathilda Duff, had been living with her children in various locations since the death of her husband in 1947. In her seventies, Archie's death gave Mathilda a new determination, a new sense of purpose. Evangeline needed her. Her granddaughters needed her. Mathilda would make the trip across the United States with Helen and Isabelle to Hickman Mills, Missouri where she would enroll Isabelle in school. Later Walter would bring Evangeline and little Helen Jean to Missouri.

In late August Evangeline watched with sadness as her mother and sister Helen left the conference grounds with Isabelle. Isabelle connected Evangeline to Archie. Though she would soon follow, that parting tore open her wounded heart, making the loss new again.

Evangeline turned her energy to readying the grounds for the coming winter. She found a couple to serve as caretakers. Along with Jake, the handyman, and John Goodmanson, who from his home in Portland accepted donations for the conference center and kept financial records, Evangeline had the local help she needed. Though these people provided support for the ministry, it felt like an insurmountable task to coordinate and supervise their work from Kansas City.

She hated to leave.

While Evangeline made preparations to move, the Cannon Beach school board notified her that they would be demolishing the old school building located across the street from the conference grounds. They unanimously voted to award the building to the center for the price of $1—if they would remove it by the required deadline. This notification surprised Evangeline, as she and Archie had bid for the building the previous winter. Hoping to use the building's lumber, they had offered the school board $1,500.00. The board refused their bid saying the amount was "too small for consideration."

Evangeline felt pressured by the school board notice. Her handyman assured her that the building couldn't be removed within the allotted time. Reluctantly, she resigned herself to missing out on the valuable lumber.

Shortly afterward Evangeline walked along the grounds with her brother, Haldane Duff, pointing out the building they almost had for $1.

"Evangeline," he said, "it would be a sin to refuse such a wonderful gift."

Haldane was not dismayed by the enormity of the project. In fact, he felt quite sure the building could be disassembled and the lumber moved within the time limits. Men from Central Bible Church in Portland were scheduled to be at the conference grounds on Labor Day Weekend. Haldane boldly asked the men's group for volunteers. To these he added recruits from his own church and arranged both a morning and afternoon shift.

As dawn rose on Labor Day, 1952, twenty-two men started work. The crews continued until dark. Hammers, wrecking bars and saws worked continually. The men sorted, stacked, and transported the lumber from the school building to the conference grounds.

In one day, they brought down the building.

The school district gave them 30 days to remove the building material. So, every weekend for four weeks, Haldane arrived in Cannon Beach with a new crew of men to remove the debris. By the end of the month, the entire pile of lumber had been transferred to conference property.

Evangeline learned much from this lesson. She saw the power of volunteer labor and recognized the hand of God guiding the work of the conference center. She also realized, in a new way, what it meant to be part of the Duff family. Certainly, they were committed to one another as brothers and sisters. Yes, they had been through difficulties and trials together. But, the Duff children were more than that.

They had become a family of burden bearers. They did more than talk about their support for one another. They lived out their beliefs. As Evangeline watched her younger brother, a minister to his own congregation, pull boards away from the pile of lumber, she realized again the treasure she had in her family. She could trust them, rely on them. Perhaps she was not as alone as she sometimes felt.

With a mixture of emotions, Evangeline left Cannon Beach with Walter and little Helen Jean. The changing seasons brought a world of changes for Evangeline. In a way, she felt as though she was leaving Archie behind. He would forever be in every building, in every bonfire, in every ocean sunset. It was almost unbearable to leave him, to leave their work, even if only for the winter.

But, at the same time she felt anticipation, excitement to be with Isabelle and Mother and her sister Helen. She looked forward to new work. New travels. New sights.

Helen had named the Christian Women's Clubs and Councils headquarters in Hickman Hills, Stonecroft. They had miraculously acquired the estate in the spring of 1952, and by July, seven women—the entire ministry staff—lived in the manse.

The solarium off the screen porch housed office space. The main floor provided the common living area. The staff used the second floor for private rooms. Evangeline, her mother, and her two daughters were given renovated servant's quarters on the third floor. The house was huge and beautifully decorated, with lush carpets and elegant furniture. Both Helen Jean and Isabelle quickly settled in. The office staff adopted them as family. Mother Duff cared for the girls and helped wherever she was needed.

Evangeline found life in Missouri a partial diversion. She enjoyed the travel her new position provided. She loved people; she loved bringing others to the Lord. She was eager to get new councils started. What a joy to be able to do the things she enjoyed most of all. She found her work with Christian Women's Clubs very satisfying.

In spite of demanding ministry, Evangeline struggled through many dark hours. Returning to Stonecroft from her long and exhausting trips, she found herself alone again. With every return, she expected to see Archie. No matter how much she knew better, she felt as if he should be waiting for her.

At Stonecroft, her children reminded her of him. The mail reminded her of him. Every delivery was filled with letters of condolence. There was nowhere in Stonecroft where she could escape her grief. During lonely Kansas nights, Isabelle often heard her mother weeping.

By mail, Evangeline did her best to care for the needs of the conference center. She wrote to the caretaker, and to the conference treasurer every week. Her brother Walter, who lived in Oregon, managed whatever she could not.

That dark winter, there were attempts to remove Evangeline as director of the conference center. Few believed that a woman could—or indeed should—direct such an important ministry. Some approached Walter, asking him to convince his sister to step down. He was the wrong person to approach. Walter believed in Evangeline and felt absolutely certain that God had chosen her to lead the conference center. Walter Duff refused to consider any objection to Evangeline's leadership—however well intentioned.

From the depth of that first Missouri winter, Evangeline made plans for an Oregon summer. She scheduled speakers, retreats, and musicians. By the time the cold gave way to thaw, Evangeline Duff McNeill had begun to see the work as her own. If God had called her, as she believed He had, then He could be trusted to help her complete the job. Even in profound grief, she found a new sense of determination and purpose.

It was this new woman, this tried and stronger woman who left the Midwest in the spring of 1953. Evangeline returned to the Oregon coast with her two daughters and her mother, determined to see God fulfill a dream at Cannon Beach.

Isabelle had endured a long, lonely winter as well. Though her grandmother tried, no one could soften the loss she felt. Her father had understood her, ridden horses with her, spent time with her. She had been ripped from the only home she knew and transplanted to the desolate, flat lands of Missouri.

Isabelle looked forward to going home.

As she traveled back to the coast, Isabelle marveled at her mother. Until his death, Isabelle had been so focused on her father, that she did not really know her mother. That had begun to change. With no one else to depend on, Isabelle began to see her mother in new ways. Amazed at her strength, Isabelle wanted to know more. Who was Evangeline Duff McNeill? What gave her the kind of grit that enabled her to overcome such incredible adversity? Curious, and lonely, Isabelle determined to answer these questions.

CHAPTER THREE

A Soul Is Born

*A*s the family buggy rounded the corner and rolled out of sight, Walter Duff turned away from his bedroom window, wondering what he would do with his time. Only mildly ill, he'd chosen to stay home while his family attended church. As he wandered downstairs, he regretted that his large Georgian-style home, with its square rooms and classical elegance, seemed strangely empty.

Normally, the obligations of the family business filled Walter's life. All three brothers had been groomed to manage the family linen mill, farms and wool holdings. A wealthy Irish family, the entire village looked to the Duffs for economic stability.

In 1892, the State Church of Northern Ireland permitted few Sunday activities. Unable to focus on business, and unwilling to spend the day idle, Walter looked around for acceptable Sunday reading. Spying a copy of the British *Christian Herald*, he settled in to the large chair by the fire with an article by the American preacher, T. DeWitt Talmadge. Soon the words riveted his attention.

When the Duff family arrived home, they found Walter charged with excitement. He described his adventure with Dr.

Talmadge. "The article made it clear," he said. "I needed forgiveness for my sins. I asked for and now possess eternal life."

Surprised by his son's revelation, his father protested. "But Walter," his father said, "of course we're Christians. Don't we give the main support to the church?"

Walter soon realized that his family could not understand the great truth of his experience. Undaunted, he continued to share his story with others. Certain his minister would understand, Walter explained what had happened. But the minister greeted his story with polite coldness.

The urge to tell others was more than Walter could resist. Soon large signs appeared on the walls of his father's mills. "Ye must be born again," they said. "PREPARE TO MEET THY GOD."

Though embarrassed by his son's zeal, James Duff chose to tolerate Walter's enthusiasm. He allowed Walter to hold spiritual meetings for the workers. Father and son continued in this way for three years, until one morning Walter entered his father's study. "Father," he said, "I must speak with you. It is of great importance."

James Duff listened carefully. "Father, I need to serve God full time—to be a pastor or an evangelist—I'm not sure which. I only know that God has called me and I must go."

This was more than the elder James Duff could endure. "No, Walter. You must stay with the firm. You are the one with energy and drive. I cannot let you go." His father was adamant, unwilling to consider his son's request.

As the days passed, James regretted the rift that had grown between them. Calling his son to him he said, "Walter, if you will remain with the firm, I will contribute the money to fully support two missionaries through your entire lifetime. You cannot do more than two people, can you?"

"But, Father," Walter answered firmly, "God has called me and I must go."

Though his father threatened to leave him penniless, Walter persisted. Though James Duff did not understand the need, his love for his son moved him to help Walter attend Bible school in Glasgow, Scotland.

Walter's commitment to full-time ministry came at great cost. When he finished school, he was largely disinherited, penniless, and separated from the approval of his family. Yet his greatest concern was not for his own loss, but for the souls of men who knew nothing of the Savior.

Returning to Ireland, Walter began to preach the gospel everywhere. Great crowds came to hear him, and many accepted his message of Good News. Clearly, people responded not to the young and inexperienced preacher but to the Holy Spirit who worked through him.

Frustrated that so many needed to hear the gospel, Walter sought a more effective way to reach people. After much prayer, he organized the Irish Christian Worker's Union, and chose dedicated, talented men and women for instruction in the Bible, and in prayer. Thus prepared, he gave the young workers many opportunities to preach throughout Ireland.

Mathilda Hamilton was one of the first young people to respond to Walter's new opportunity. Orphaned in her early teens, she lived in with a maternal aunt. There, Mathilda came to know her Savior. In spite of her difficult life, she had committed herself to full-time missions work and applied to serve as a missionary to Africa. Considered too frail and delicate for the African climate, she was turned down.

Determined to serve, Mathilda applied to the Christian Worker's Union where she met Walter Duff. Her own deep love for the Savior was evident and attractive to Walter. She too was Irish. Her deep brown eyes were lovely, and he found her dark hair and tiny figure attractive. Together their zeal for evangelism multiplied. After some time, the two became engaged.

On March 1, 1901, Mathilda Hamilton married Walter Duff. They took a brief honeymoon in Loch Lomond, Scotland and returned to their work.

In the early twentieth century, a great wave of revival passed through the British Isles. Unfortunately, mainline churches were not receptive to evangelists. Because they viewed the young speakers as untrained, the Presbyterian Church absolutely refused to host the Union's preachers. Undaunted, the Irish Christian Worker's Union held meetings in local community halls and schoolhouses. Walter and Mathilda rented large country homes, near enough to travel by bicycle, where they hosted the Union preachers.

In Ireland, large numbers of people responded to the gospel. Walter planned conventions at resorts such as Giant's Causeway and Portrush. To transport enormous crowds from the city to the seaside resorts, he hired special trains. Often as many as five thousand people attended, traveling great distances for a single meeting.

This spiritual awakening was so great that it was said, "There is hardly a person in all Northern Ireland who cannot explain the simplicity of the grace of God." The revival provided continuing financial support for the training of the Union's young missionaries.

In the midst of organizing and training young evangelists, Walter and Mathilda began their own family. Together they had four children. Helen, the oldest, Alexandra (who came to be known as Evangeline Duff), Walter Jr., and Olive.

In Ireland, Mathilda continued to struggle with her health. Occasionally she was forced to spend long periods confined to bed. In spite of these limitations, her love for her children, combined with her deep love for Jesus, made her an extraordinary mother. Every evening the children gathered around her bed for story time.

She read them a Bible story or told them of a missionary's adventure. As soon as she finished the children would chorus, "Tell it again, Mother!" Using all her energy, she embellished the story, adding theatrical details. The children loved those evenings.

With many large and beautiful rooms, the great houses rented by the Duff family were situated on beautifully landscaped grounds. Mathilda often took the children for long walks along the country hedges. An artist herself (Mathilda had displayed many of her early paintings in London), her eye for color, beauty and texture was a source of much discussion and instruction for the children. Together they identified wildflowers and bulbs while enjoying fresh air and exercise.

From her own family, Mathilda brought a great love and talent for music. Her father had been a church choir director and her sister a famous singer, known as "the sweet singer of Londonderry." Mathilda played the auto harp and the small family organ. She shared her passion for music with the children, and as youngsters they sang many hymns together around the little organ.

Over time, the young preachers trained by Reverend Duff found pastoral positions all over the English-speaking world. Many, who immigrated to the United States, wrote to Walter urging him to come to America. "There is multiplied opportunity here," they assured him. Though he repeatedly refused, still the letters came.

Gradually, he began to consider such a move, wondering if conditions across the sea might improve Mathilda's fragile health. After much prayer, Reverend Walter Duff finally decided to emigrate to the United States, traveling alone to find a pastoral position. After settling in, he planned to make arrangements for Mathilda and the children.

Walter found it very difficult to leave his young family. He had never been separated from Mathilda. His oldest child was only nine. In spite of his reluctance, Walter sensed the strong hand of God moving him toward the United States.

Through an Irish pastor in Minneapolis, Walter found and accepted the pastorate of the International Falls Baptist Church. A small community of about 1000 Swedish immigrants, International Falls, Minnesota was located very near the Canadian border.

The Rainy River separated International Falls from its Canadian counterpart, Fort Francis, Ontario. This community too, desperately needed a pastor. After agreeing to supply both pulpits, Walter rented an old wood frame house large enough for his family.

Not long after reaching America, Walter Duff began the habit of preaching in the American church on Sunday mornings, rowing himself across the river, and preaching at the Canadian church on Sunday evenings. As soon as he could afford the passage, he made plans to bring his family to the United States.

At last the perfect opportunity presented itself. *Unsinkable*, they called her. *The fastest ship afloat.* Launched in 1911, built by Harland-Wolf in Walter's own beloved Belfast, the HMS *Titanic* was the hottest news of the year. Her enormous size, speed, and unsurpassed grandeur convinced Walter to purchase passage on the *Titanic's* inaugural cruise, scheduled for April 11, 1912. This remarkable ship would surely bring Walter's beloved family swiftly and safely to his side. With great anticipation, he made arrangements for their journey.

At home in Ireland, Mathilda desperately missed Walter. Though he had provided a servant to help her with the children, having her husband on another continent made her responsibility a serious burden.

When Walter wired her with plans for her travel to America, Mathilda was thrilled, anxious to end their long separation. She filled the long, lonely hours by sorting and packing their household goods. Eagerly, the young family looked forward to the day of their departure.

However, in February 1912, news of an English coal strike dampened Mathilda's plans. The *Titanic*, scheduled to leave from Southampton, England, traveled at such speeds that she could not cross the Atlantic without a full load of coal. The company announced that her departure would be delayed until the strike ended.

Walter, determined not to postpone his family's arrival, wired again. "Change plans," he wrote, "Sail from Londonderry."

Not only would another ship sail immediately, but by leaving from Londonderry, Mathilda would not have to manage the long trip from Ireland to Southampton with four young children by herself. She made new plans, wired Walter, and purchased passage on the steamship *Scandinavia*, a ship of only 17,000 tons.

It disappointed her to miss sailing on the century's "greatest engineering feat." Knowing that trips abroad would not be a regular part of their lifestyle, Mathilda felt that she had lost a singular opportunity. She had heard of the *Titanic*'s rich interiors, and private decks. All of Europe had watched as the 66,000-ton vessel neared completion.

The ship would sail with the world's wealthiest families aboard. The passenger list included John Jacob Astor, the Vanderbilt's and many others. The largest manmade object in the world, the *Titanic* was filled with hand-carved wood, electric chandeliers, ballrooms and restaurants—all of these part of a wonderful opportunity she would never again experience. Eager to join her husband, Mathilda swallowed her disappointment. She determined to joyfully cross the Atlantic on whatever ship was available.

At last, spring brought the day of departure. Though the *Scandinavia* was a small ship, it was freshly painted. The family found their tiny quarters comfortable. Once at sea, however, they were plagued by seasickness. Mathilda and her daughter Alexandra, nearly eight, spent most of the trip confined to their cabin. The other children, under big sister Helen's watchful eye, had free run of the ship. And run they did, with endless deck races and adventures. Before long, they became friends with both crew and passengers. Mathilda was grateful that Helen was a capable child. She was even more grateful to have the children away from the cabin.

Despite her hope that the passage would be swift, the ship traveled slowly. Three days, five days, seven days. The trip dragged on. Her seasickness did not abate. Then unexpectedly, in mid-Atlantic, the ship began stopping frequently. Checking in with their mother, the children reported the strange actions and worried expressions of the crew. "Taking water temperature," Helen reported, "to watch for icebergs." What began as a leisurely passage slowed to a snail's pace.

Suddenly the engines stopped again.

This time, the children brought even more disappointing news. Because of the coal strike, the *Scandinavia* set sail from Ireland without a full fuel supply. The frequent stops and slow passage had completely used up their coal. Thus they were forced to wait mid-ocean for more coal.

Somehow, the days passed and they were underway again. After 14 long days the ship reached Halifax, Nova Scotia, where passengers bound for Canada disembarked. It was not until they docked that Mathilda learned of the *Titanic* disaster.

The *Titanic* had left England long after the *Scandinavia* sailed. Because of her speed, the *Titanic* had nearly caught up with the *Scandinavia* when she sank. The captain of the ship carrying the Duff family had heard of the sinking mid-voyage on the new Marconi invention called the "wireless."

It was the shocking catastrophe of the *Titanic* that prompted him to test carefully for icebergs. The *Scandinavia* had sailed only three hundred miles from the place where the *Titanic* sank.

The news overwhelmed Mathilda. All of Halifax was draped in mourning as a reminder of the tragedy. By the time the *Scandinavia* docked, two vessels were appointed to leave Halifax to recover the bodies of *Titanic*'s victims. Along the docks of the shipping line, stacked coffins waited to be loaded onto the search ships. Of the nearly 1700 passengers and crew on the *Titanic*, only 800 survived. Most of these were the wealthy first class passengers.

The depth of the story had only begun to unfold when Mathilda reached Nova Scotia. Twenty lifeboats had sailed on the *Titanic*, not nearly enough for everyone on board. Most of the lifeboats were launched nearly empty. Though the third class fare for Mathilda's family would have cost $20, only a handful of the Irish immigrants sailing third class survived.

Looking out over the stacks of coffins, Mathilda felt deep gratitude for God's protection. She brushed away tears as she prayed for those involved in the *Titanic* disaster. Through something as commonplace as a coal strike, God had redirected her family and saved their lives. In spite of her exhaustion and seasickness, she could not help but wonder as she looked at each of her own children. For what divine purpose had they been so miraculously spared?

Chapter Four

The New Land

W hen Mathilda and her family reached Boston, Massachusetts, the last stop for the *Scandinavia*, the port was filled with ships. The streets bustled with new immigrants. With great relief Mathilda and her four children disembarked their floating home and made their way to the customs office. Shuffling the children through, Mathilda faced an irritable customs officer who made fun of their traditionally long family names. "Who do you think you are?" he smirked. "Royalty?"

She turned tearful eyes away from him. Seeing her fatigue, and the burden of her solitary crossing, the officer stamped her papers quickly. "Ah, lady, you have an honest face."

Mathilda discovered that all the hotel rooms in Boston were taken. Exhausted, she eventually found space in the lobby of a city hotel, where she and the children spent the night. The next morning they boarded a train for the Midwest.

Their reunion, in the train station at International Falls, held more joy than any Walter had ever experienced. Embracing each child in turn, and finally Mathilda, Walter's eyes spilled over with relief and gratitude.

All over the world, people had been mesmerized by the details of the *Titanic*'s sinking. After the first news of the disaster, Walter had read every word of every newspaper he could find. He had followed the first accounts of "slight damage—all passengers saved," grateful for God's grace. But, when the true dimension of the tragedy was revealed, Walter too had been completely overwhelmed by God's supernatural protection for his family.

Determined that his young family would never be separated again, Walter loaded his family and their belongings into a horse and buggy and started out for their home in this new land.

International Falls, Minnesota, a town of about 1000 people was located 275 miles due north of Minneapolis. It was a land of lakes, rivers and deep forests—a wilderness that terrified Mathilda, having grown up in the dense urban area of Ireland. She took some comfort in discovering that Walter had found a home in town. Not only was the land different, but the people bewildered her as well. The Irish were a private and close-mouthed people. She found it very difficult to adjust to the outspoken and sometimes crude manners of the Swedish immigrants.

With time, as she found her neighbors kind and thoughtful, she came to value them deeply. The following year passed quickly for the Duff family. The two congregations on either side of the border loved their new pastor and his talented wife. The family enjoyed church picnics and long walks amidst the deep forests. The children played in many vacant lots. Tall, lithe, Native Americans were part of their daily experience.

Close friendships developed. An Episcopal minister befriended the family with frequent visits and gifts. A lonesome bachelor, he enjoyed the company of the lively Irish family. He often brought fresh maple syrup. On one visit, he taught the children how to roll clumps of syrup in the snow, and shape and pull the syrup into candy.

By the time winter took hold of Minnesota the Duffs looked forward with delightful anticipation to the spring arrival of another Duff baby. The children were especially excited—at last a child born in the United States—a real American.

On May 21, 1913, Mathilda gave birth to Haldane Duff in the small rural hospital located only a few blocks from their International Falls home. Every day, Helen led her brothers and sisters to visit their mother and the new baby. After the long hospitalization, the children were delighted to have their mother home again.

By now the children were old enough to read, and Mathilda organized what she called the "evening reader." While the children did the dinner dishes, the reader would keep them entertained by reading works of famous authors. Taking turns as reader, all the children grew to love the writing of Charles Dickens, Robert Louis Stevenson and many others. As the months passed, the Duff family began to feel more truly a part of their new surroundings.

In the fall of 1913 Walter became greatly concerned about Mathilda. The severe Midwestern winters had begun to take a toll on her health. Frequently confined to bed, her fragile condition worsened. Helen and Alexandra, only ten and nine, took over as many household responsibilities as they could manage.

Walter began to fear for Mathilda's life, asking everyone he knew, "Where in the United States is there a mild climate like Ireland?" His research pointed him toward the Pacific Northwest. Friends in his Fort Francis church put him in contact with an Irish pastor in Oregon City, Oregon who arranged for Portland's Calvary Baptist church to hear Reverend Walter Duff. In 1914 the church called Walter to become their pastor.

That spring, the Duff family again packed their belongings and traveled by train to Hood River, Oregon where Reverend Duff filled a temporary pastorate waiting for the Portland position to open. By fall, the Duffs settled into Portland and their second American pastorate.

The mild Oregon climate was everything Walter Duff hoped; but he found himself deeply disappointed in the Christians living on the west coast. Walter's heart beat for the unsaved, and try as he would, he could not persuade his congregation to take up the job of winning souls.

To him, all of Portland lived in what he considered a "spiritual slump."

Everywhere Reverend Duff went, he found people who needed to hear about Jesus. Though others refused to share their faith, Walter determined to do everything he could to spread the Good News. With this in mind, one afternoon in 1918, Reverend Duff took his son Walter Jr. with him on a streetcar into downtown Portland.

As they disembarked on Alder street, the older Duff spoke. "Walter," he said, "there are men on this street who need to know about Jesus." He bent down to meet young Walter's eyes. "And we are going to find a way to tell them. We are going to rent some space in a building, and hold services and have literature. It will be just what these men need. Today we are going to find the space God has for us to use."

So together, father and son tramped the sidewalks until at last they found available office space at 3rd and Alder. Walter rented the building and began making plans for his new project.

Within months, Walter's church grew into one of Portland's largest and most prestigious churches. At the same time he managed a flourishing ministry to street people. At "Hope Hall" Walter sold religious literature and held both Sunday afternoon and evening services. Eventually, he taught several Bible classes there and began publishing a small weekly paper.

Each week, the Duff children accompanied their parents to Hope Hall. Reverend Duff was a delightful and energetic preacher. No one admired him more than his own five children who faithfully took their places on the front row.

To the Oregonians in Reverend Duff's congregation, their new Irish pastor seemed a different sort—he had such a serious regard for his faith. His straightforward zeal surprised them. Though some were offended, most were completely won over by his delightful sense of humor and deep love for people.

In the midst of this first year in Portland, Mathilda became ill again. Confined to bed, she continued to love and lead her family. Even with much rest, her condition grew worse. At last she and Walter returned to the doctor.

All of Portland seemed damp and grey when finally the two returned home. The children recognized fear in their mother's eyes as she came in the parlor door. With tender care, Father prepared her tea and carried her upstairs to bed. Somehow, the children knew. Silence filled the house as they waited for Father to come downstairs.

"Children," he said gathering them together around the large kitchen table, "the doctor says your mother has consumption. He says she will not live much longer. Mother is afraid because your grandmother died of consumption."

Walter paused to let the children understand his words. Through his own tears, he looked at each face in turn. "But," he continued, "the doctor does not know about Jesus. So, we will pray. We will ask Jesus to spare your mother's life. We will ask and believe," he said, "and then we will trust Him."

So as the rain fell outside, small tears fell inside. Together five children and one desperate husband prayed earnestly for the life of the woman so precious to them.

Darkness fell. The rain stopped. But the prayers continued. At last, Walter lit the hall lamps and led his sleepy tribe to bed. Lovingly he said goodnight to each. "Jesus hears our prayers," he promised. "We will see."

Weeks passed. Mathilda's strength slowly returned. Gradually it seemed that the worst was over. A grand celebration accompanied her first dinner in the big kitchen.

With the joy of Mathilda's returning health, Walter focused again on the work of the church and of Hope Hall. Things were happening downtown. People responded to his messages. Walter found that many were eager to know more about the Good News he proclaimed. Once again his love for evangelistic work came to life. He began to feel the desire to leave the pastorate and concentrate on reaching the lost.

But with such a large family to support, how could he move into full time evangelism? How could he leave the security of salary and parsonage? With much prayer, Reverend Walter Duff Sr. resigned from Calvary Baptist. If God was the source of this new direction, how could he do anything else?

Chapter Five

Operation Evangelism

꧁꧂

*D*etermined to provide for his family as he followed the Lord's leading, Walter searched for answers. Eventually, he located a tiny church on Portland's east side. In need of a pastor, Tabernacle Baptist had been closed for years.

The Oregon State Baptist Committee agreed to let the Duffs live in the church's small parsonage if Walter would fill the pulpit and reopen the small church. In addition, they would contribute $20 per month in salary.

For almost two years he occupied the pulpit of Tabernacle Baptist and continued his work at Hope Hall. At the same time, he began holding evangelistic meetings in nearby communities. At first, he traveled along the west coast of Washington, Oregon and British Columbia. His ministry was well received, and before long Walter began including the children in his work.

Never greatly concerned with formal education, Walter would take the children out of school to travel with him. Helen—in her late teens—was the first to come along. Later Walter Jr. and Alexandra joined them as well. Mathilda, who wanted her children to finish school, always found some reason for one of the children to stay at home with her. In this way, each completed high school, though the long absences made Alexandra nearly twenty before she graduated.

Out of his great passion for evangelism, Father Duff trained each of the children in every area of public ministry, believing they must be fully equipped to take on the work that so consumed him. Before long, they could all preach, lead the song service, and play any number of hymns. From her home in Oregon, Mathilda supported the team by choosing special music. She trained the teenagers in instrumental and vocal duets and trios. As they were able, each of the children entered full-time evangelistic work.

One afternoon, shortly after returning from a trip with her father, Alexandra entered his study. "What is it, Alec?" father asked.

"Father, I need to speak to you of something important." She steadied herself. "I want to be called Evangeline. When we travel together, you use your pet names for me in public. I am too old to be called 'Alec,' Father. My middle name is Evangeline, and I want to use it."

"Certainly, Evangeline." Father's eyes smiled at her. His daughter had grown into a lovely young woman.

Under Father's watchful eye, the children's talents were carefully developed. Together they blended into a perfectly orchestrated, wonderfully effective team. After some time, Walter Jr. began to hold services on his own. The three younger sisters joined forces to become the Duff Sisters Gospel Trio. Helen often preached and Evangeline led the song services.

In each location, the Duff sisters provided an afternoon children's program, training the local children to participate in the evening service. Whether in a dramatic presentation, or in music, families flocked to see the evening "performance" of their children.

Early on, the Duff Sisters Trio focused on rural villages without church programs of their own. Often these communities had old abandoned church buildings. The girls obtained permission to use those buildings and spent whatever time and energy was necessary to clean and ready the auditorium for services.

Though it took many hours, the sisters also chose to personally invite families in nearby homes to their services. Evangeline managed the trio's publicity. She designed fliers, wrote newspaper releases, and was constantly on the lookout for clever ways to draw townspeople to their services. Olive and Helen never knew what to expect from Evangeline. But one of her latest techniques had completely surprised them. Evangeline fit their little truck with long poles supporting a great banner announcing the trio.

"What is that for?" Helen asked.

"We'll just have ourselves a little musical parade," Evangeline said, her eyes merry with the fun of it. "Only we will be the whole parade!"

"Evangeline!" Olive gasped, "When? Where?"

"I think noon would be good," she replied, "right down Main Street." The three young girls played their instruments as they worked their way down Main Street. Talented, energetic and attractive in their tailored blue serge dresses with white collars and cuffs, the plan worked. That evening, many townspeople attended their service.

Because they planned programs filled with charm and humor, the sisters had no difficulty filling the small churches night after night. Many came to know the Savior they so exuberantly served. Among denominations, word passed quickly that this young group effectively brought entire communities to Christ.

Invitations to other towns and churches eventually exceeded their ability to respond. Bigger churches in larger cities began to request their services. Soon the Duff Sisters Trio held citywide meetings in large churches up and down the west coast.

Routinely, the sisters made it a priority to greet their guests after each service. One evening in Eureka, California,

Helen found a small piece of paper folded and pressed into her hand. Surprised, and without any clue as to its importance, she slipped the paper into her pocket. *Later*, she thought, *I'll see what this is.*

That night, as they traveled to their room, Helen passed the small paper to Olive. "Girls, look," Olive said. "It's a check. And I think it is made out for $500!"

In the early 1920s such a sum was so enormous, so unheard of, that Helen immediately pulled their little car off to the side of the road. In the dark, the three girls got out and held the check up in the headlamps. Olive had not been mistaken. The check clearly read five hundred dollars.

Together, they considered the situation. Surely someone had meant to write the check for five dollars. What would they do? The solution was simple. The next day they would go together and return the check. With the matter settled, they went to bed.

The next day the three girls began looking for the donor. With some persistence, they arrived at a tiny shack located near a county road-building project. On that hot day, gritty dust hung in the air and coated every item in the little hut.

In spite of their surroundings, R.G. and Evelyn LeTourneau greeted the girls with a bubbling enthusiasm that refreshed them all the way to the soul. "No, the check was no mistake," R.G. assured them. "It was an expression of thanks for the great job you three are doing." And so, in spite of the heat and the dust, the sisters began what became a long friendship between the two families.

After a time, the five young people rented a house together. The rental provided respite for the LeTourneaus, away from the dust of the road project. For the girls, the house became the base of operation for their traveling ministry.

The friendship blossomed.

In this house, the LeTourneaus and the Duff sisters agreed to take a break from their work to study at the Bible Institute of Los Angeles (BIOLA). In 1926 with the financial support of the LeTourneaus, the group traveled south for the fall term.

Before long Helen desperately missed evangelistic work. Studying, she felt, took valuable time from the more productive work of winning souls. Even at school, she continued to receive invitations to conduct services. Reluctantly she left her two sisters behind and resumed evangelistic ministry.

Olive and Evangeline, however, loved school. They studied hard and were successful in their classes. They attended the Church of the Open Door in Los Angeles, pastored by the renowned Scottish preacher John McNeill. Known as the Scottish "Spurgeon," McNeill had served the three largest congregations in the United States. His son, Archie McNeill, also attended BIOLA. Many a weekend found a large group of students at the McNeill home for an evening of fun.

Soon Archie, a tall, roundish young man with a thick Scottish brogue became enamored with Evangeline Duff. In the European way, he approached her about the prospect. Because he was new in the United States (having only recently immigrated from Scotland), Evangeline rejected his approach.

"He's nice enough, and lots of fun," she told her sister Olive. "It's just that he's so un-American. He's definitely not for me!"

By the end of their first term, R.G. LeTourneau took a job on a Florida road project, urging Olive and Evangeline to follow along. The girls had no desire to travel to Florida, and no funds to continue school. So, with a shrug of the shoulders, they left BIOLA and returned to the work they knew so well. Happy to be together again, they joined Helen and her full schedule of meetings.

A short time later, a classically trained pianist named Charles Huddleston joined the girls. His family background was similar to the Duffs, and from the moment he joined them, he fit in. His strong and powerful approach to the keyboard gave balance to Evangeline's charm and vocal abilities.

Pastors recommended the team saying, "There isn't a soul in the house who can resist the fun of the singing." As the crowds continued to come and cities and churches continued to request their services, the four traveled together.

After a church service in San Jose, California, the girls were invited to the pastor's home. Many from the congregation were there, including a handsome young banker who seemed especially glad to meet Helen. Though the girls left town soon after the meeting, the resourceful banker, Elwood Baugh, often followed them to meetings in distant towns, just to visit with Helen. In spite of a difficult courtship, he pursued and won her love.

On January 23, 1928 Helen married Elwood Baugh. Unfortunately, the schedule for the Duff Trio was so busy that it was nearly six months before Helen could return to San Jose to live with her new husband.

Before long, Charles Huddleston, the new pianist, decided that he was especially fond of another of the Duff sisters. He and Olive were married on January 26, 1930. The newlyweds settled in California.

With her two sisters happily married, and the trio no more, Evangeline made plans of her own. Walter Duff Jr. asked Evangeline to join him in his evangelistic work. She was glad to help her brother. Haldane, the youngest Duff, occasionally joined Walter and Evangeline, once again creating a Duff Irish Trio. The three siblings traveled a broad area of the country together. Their talent, hard work, and commitment to prayer made them a successful team.

Part of their success came from the Great Depression. With poverty rampant, people had almost no money and nothing to do. There were few distractions in the hard working lives of rural folks. Evangelistic meetings were exciting happenings in small and large communities alike. Crowds continued to attend.

Though others found the days economically difficult, Walter, Evangeline, and Haldane were never in need. While other evangelists earned reputations as fraudulent scoundrels, the Duffs were very careful to outline their financial policy before they agreed to come to a community.

They would come for the amount of the nightly offering only. There would be no promotion. No "Love Offering." They would take just one quiet offering at each meeting. People found this agreeable. And never, in all the turbulent economic times of the Great Depression, did the Duff Evangelistic Trio find themselves wanting.

Eventually, Haldane left them to return to college and Walter and Evangeline took an engagement in Roseburg, Oregon. Rumor had it that a large concert harp, located on the second floor of an old theatre building, had been retained in lieu of rent from a passing theatre company. Evangeline normally accompanied herself using a small Irish harp. *What an exciting possibility,* she thought, *to own a concert harp.* It would make a wonderful addition to their music program.

Though many had tried unsuccessfully to buy the beautiful, full-sized Wurlitzer harp, Walter and Evangeline made arrangements with the owner to view the instrument. Now more than 20 years old, they were taken with its beautiful condition. They asked the owner to sell the instrument on contract with no success. Subsequent visits, covered with prayer, seemed to change his mind—especially when he understood their intended purpose. He agreed to sell.

Two hundred dollars was an enormous investment in those times. Faithfully, Walter and Evangeline made monthly payments of $10 or $20 until at last the harp belonged to them. With much gratitude, Walter and Evangeline loaded the enormous instrument onto the trailer which would be its traveling home.

They were the Duff Trio again!

Together Walter and Evangeline traveled to city after city. As a direct result of their ministry, large numbers of people decided to trust in the forgiveness of Christ. Everywhere they encouraged believers to live fully for Christ.

Together constantly, Walter and Evangeline became the closest of friends. He came to respect her tremendous musical talent, her ability to communicate the gospel, and her head for administration. She admired his preaching ability, as well as his unaffected leadership and practical problem solving. Few brothers and sisters had such a unique opportunity to work together. They treasured their time together.

Then in 1933, Walter and Evangeline held services in Dallas, Oregon where, in the Methodist church, Walter was introduced to a charming and lovely schoolteacher. Though she had been raised in the church, Edith Dunn was never quite sure of her own salvation. In these services, she came to truly understand what Christ had done for her. It was a life-changing realization.

Walter left Dallas. But,he didn't forget the lovely teacher. Eighteen months later, Edith Dunn received her first letter from the handsome evangelist. He was concerned about the difference in their ages, and he wanted to give her time to grow and develop her own talents. A long courtship followed.

The Duff family received so many invitations to conduct meetings that Walter and Evangeline occasionally separated to meet the many requests. By 1936, Evangeline traveled with Naomi Van Cleave, a friend of Walter's who had studied dramatic presentation in college. She added recitations and dramatic readings to the services. Evangeline led the music and preached the messages. They were happy traveling together, and decided to purchase a mobile home and continue to work. Finding a truck with a homemade shelter, the two women set off to win the world to Christ.

Their timing proved perfect. In June of 1936, Evangeline's brother Walter Duff Jr., married Edith Dunn. The newlyweds chose to work together. Eventually, Walter settled into pastoral work.

Though Evangeline greatly missed Walter, she was happy for him. Walter and Edith delighted in one another. Still, some tiny bit of sadness persisted. She could not help but wonder if she would ever experience the happiness her brother had found.

As Evangeline continued her work with Naomi, she found deep contentment in the results. Still, she could not escape the question that so badgered her quiet moments:

Does God have someone special for me?

CHAPTER SIX

Love at Last

In November of 1937, Naomi and Evangeline, now 33, began to work their way toward San Jose, California where Evangeline's sister Helen and her husband Elwood Baugh would host a family Thanksgiving. Evangeline's parents, staying in Helen's guest house, were enjoying a mild California winter. Haldane, now attending BIOLA, had invited school friends to join the holiday festivities. Walter Jr. brought Edith down from Oregon. The women looked forward to a wonderful family gathering.

They spent their first evening together catching up. Haldane's friends included his girlfriend, a skilled pianist, and their old friend Archie McNeill. After dinner music filled the big house, and hymn followed hymn amid laughter and gaiety. Late in the evening, Archie, an accomplished vocalist, reluctantly agreed to sing for them.

As his rich baritone voice filled the living room, Evangeline found herself deeply moved by his beautiful rendition of the old hymn, "Son of My Soul." It was more than his performance that caught her attention. Somewhere deep in the heart of the singer something had changed.

When she had last seen Archie, Evangeline was quite certain that he had made no real commitment to Christ. But as she listened to him sing, she realized that every phrase carried the deep devotion of the singer. She could not mistake the transformation. His was a Christ-filled life. Even as she listened Evangeline found a deep love springing up inside her.

Over the long weekend the six young people spent much time together. Each day they went sightseeing, once to the mountains, once to the conservatory, and always with a large picnic lunch. Every evening they returned to a meal prepared by Helen and Mathilda. For their contribution, Archie and Evangeline volunteered to wash dishes.

Alone in the kitchen, the two enjoyed much conversation. In the eight years since they attended BIOLA together, Archie's father had resigned his Los Angeles church and returned to preach in the British Isles. Because Evangeline had not heard anything more from him, she assumed that Archie had gone to Europe with his family. But the story he told over dishes that weekend was quite different.

Leaving BIOLA, Archie began to earnestly study music and voice with the goal of a career in opera. It was a long, difficult pursuit, fraught with the frustration of financial troubles. He worked hard to gain recognition in the entertainment industry.

Then Archie had joined a wildly diverse group of young men, each a soloist in his own right. They called themselves "The International Four." After much work, and generous critics, they eventually gained success in Hollywood. Engagements, money, bright lights and notoriety were at last his. Archie was on his way.

While he pursued fame, Archie also served as the bass soloist for a Long Beach church choir. Special services, conducted by Dr. John G. Mitchell, required his nightly attendance. At the end of one service, late in the week, Archie realized, "I am living a lie—son of the famous Dr. John McNeill—a church member, a soloist—but not a Christian."

Just as he had after every service, that night Dr. Mitchell gave an altar call. Archie hesitated a long time before responding. While he heard the call to salvation, he also recognized the Holy Spirit calling him to a life of full-time service. He could not respond to one call while ignoring the other. It seemed like hours passed as he wrestled with his decision. In the end, only moments later, Archie came forward. His heart responded with a resounding "yes."

The decision, though difficult to make, had an overwhelming affect on his heart. Suddenly in love with the Lord, Archie told everyone about his newfound happiness.

In spite of this, he found it more difficult to tell the other members of the quartet. At last they were entertaining the biggest names in Hollywood. How could he throw away such opportunity for some Christian service as yet unknown?

He was sure they would never understand.

Later, after a night of entertaining the stars, the quartet was invited to an exclusive Hollywood nightclub. As the night progressed, so did the drinking and carousing. The sight became embarrassing and uncomfortable to Archie. As the son of a minister, Archie knew he didn't belong. The brazen drunkenness of the evening gave him the courage he needed to make the break.

His prediction proved correct. After working so hard to succeed, no one in the quartet could understand Archie's willingness to throw it all away.

Archie felt disappointment as well. With nothing left of his old life, how should he follow the Lord? In spite of his uncertainty, he knew the Lord would show him in due time.

Soon after breaking with the quartet, an old friend of Archie's parents heard about his conversion. With some effort she found him in Los Angeles. He would need training to ready himself for ministry, she thought. Would he consider returning to BIOLA under financial sponsorship?

Archie, hungry for God's divine direction, eagerly accepted the teacher's kind offer. This was the new and improved Archie McNeill that Haldane Duff invited home for the holidays. This was the man who helped Evangeline dry dishes.

After the holiday, from the driveway of Helen's home, Evangeline waved at Archie and Haldane as they headed back to BIOLA. She sighed, disappointed that the weekend had ended so quickly. She wished she could continue her new friendship with Archie McNeill; but this decision was not hers to make.

Keeping her thoughts to herself, Evangeline returned to the house. She and Naomi planned to stay in San Jose until Christmas. Daily Evangeline watched the mail, hoping for some contact with Archie.

At last a letter arrived—but it held only a thank you note for her parents.

Evangeline began to pray. This new interest in Archie was more than she could handle on her own. As with everything, she submitted her hopes and desires, concerns and fears to her Lord in prayer. "Bring him back," she prayed fervently, "but only as a sign of your approval. Lord, if this is not for me—may I never see him again!" It took courage to pray that way. She already loved Archie, and to see him again without having God's approval would be too painful.

Evangeline waited.

At last she received a letter from Haldane. Having noticed her interest in Archie, Haldane wrote to let her know that Archie was writing regularly to a girl in Canada. "Don't think another thing about him," her brother advised. "He isn't available."

Deeply disappointed, Evangeline prayed more earnestly. God knew how she felt. Certainly, He could handle all the details.

⌘

The end of the Thanksgiving holiday had been difficult for Archie as well. Evangeline was a remarkable woman. She was mature, energetic and attractive. She brought deep integrity to her relationship with her Savior. Evangeline too had changed since her days at BIOLA, and in every way, Archie found the changes more attractive.

Evangeline was not the first woman for whom Archie felt attraction. In the years since he first attended BIOLA, he had already broken an engagement. The experience troubled him. He'd grown so much since those days. He desperately wanted to follow God's lead in his life. Since God brought him to BIOLA through dramatic circumstances, Archie reasoned that God could clearly confirm His direction in choosing a wife.

So Archie resolved not to contact Evangeline. Instead, he began to pray. He earnestly desired to return to San Jose and Evangeline for Christmas; but he had no transportation, and no money. In the midst of the Great Depression, with more than 500 miles separating them, this seemed like an impossible wish.

He prayed. "Lord, will you provide a way? If you don't, I will know with certainty that she is not your choice for me." Archie tried not to entertain doubt, though he realized that because of a Christmas choir tour, he would not be able to work during the holidays. Without finances of his own, Archie watched his mail carefully.

Normally, his family remembered him with a check at Christmas time. But, this season, he found the mailbox empty.

When the tour ended, all of Archie's closest friends left for home. As the days passed, Archie's hope for a trip to San Jose seemed to slip away. In the echoing silence of the campus, he returned to his room alone. The last few cheery good-byes of his classmates only deepened his despair. He would not make any step toward San Jose unless God led the way. He had prayed this way; he would stick with his prayer.

In San Jose, Evangeline occupied herself with Christmas preparations, but her thoughts never drifted far from Archie. Christmas vacation arrived and Haldane came to Helen's home alone. Though disappointed, Evangeline greeted him warmly. When they were alone together, Haldane told Evangeline, "I know you care for him, Evangeline. But you must change your heart. He is in love with someone else."

Evangeline fought with her emotions. *God knows,* she thought.

⌘

With sinking disappointment, Archie hid in his room. A knock on his dormitory door interrupted his thoughts. "Archie," his friend said, "I heard you might be interested in a trip north. I'm headed for San Francisco. But, I'm so tired, there's no way I can drive up there myself. If you'll drive— you can come along for free."

Hours later, Archie drove north—toward San Jose. Toward Evangeline.

That night, alone with his thoughts, Archie realized that he still did not know what would happen. What about Evangeline? They had shared no affection. She had given no indication. Did she care for him?

She had not even written to him. What if his love were unreturned? In the dark, he shook his head. How foolish he would feel.

⌘

Evangeline spent her days helping Mother and Helen. But even Christmas decorating and baking didn't provide the usual fun. In spite of Haldane's warning, Evangeline's thoughts returned to Archie. Did he care? Would he return? Each thought prompted her to prayer. Her life partner would have to be God's choice. Over and over again, she placed her hope for the future in the hands of her loving God. For 33 years, God had met her every need. Certainly she could trust Him now.

Then one morning, just two days before Christmas, Evangeline answered a knock at Helen's front door. There stood Archie, a giant of a young man, his hair disheveled, and his eyes red from sleeplessness, a bright smile expressing his happiness. Suppressing her excitement, Evangeline escorted him inside.

"Something to eat, and a good rest is what you need," Evangeline assured him. As he ate, she went off to prepare his room. Later, striving to appear natural, she closed the door to Archie's room, her heart full of gratitude for God's guiding hand. Clearly, His approval rested on her choice.

As Archie slept, Evangeline contemplated the upcoming gift exchange. Finding her mother in the guesthouse, she asked for advice concerning the appropriateness of a gift for Archie. With Mathilda's encouragement, Evangeline slipped away to select a shaving kit. She carried it home, wrapped it lovingly and hid it beneath the tree.

Suddenly Christmas was exciting again.

Archie rose refreshed and happy, eager to join the festivities. But the sight of so many gifts under the tree concerned him. Pulling Evangeline aside, he said sheepishly, "I am not able to participate in gift giving. Perhaps I should not join you."

"But Archie, we want you with us," she said, assuring him that her family certainly understood the financial circumstances of depression-era students. A gift was not expected. After all, this was an exchange of gifts between family members.

Helen and Elwood had remembered all the guests with gifts. Archie had brought a box of chocolates for the family. When Archie was given Evangeline's gift, he looked surprised. But anyone could see how much her thoughtfulness pleased him. He thanked Evangeline warmly and gently chided her about their earlier conversation.

The evening continued as before, but something was different. Evangeline sensed Archie's eyes following her every movement. After evening tea, when dessert dishes had been cleared and the last of the wrapping paper had been burned, it was time to say good night. Archie asked if he might walk Evangeline out to the guesthouse.

Along the path in the garden, he caught her elbow and turned her toward him. "Could we talk just a while?" Even in the moonlight she recognized the concern and earnestness in his face. With careful detail, he relayed his prayer of the last five weeks. "I wanted to return, to contact you. But I was so afraid that you might not share the feelings I have for you." His words came in a rush. Tight features betrayed his anticipation. Taking a deep breath he began again, "But tonight, I think I know. Tell me, do you care?"

How Evangeline treasured his tender expression on that chilly December night. What joy to know that God had so divinely brought them together. Yes, Evangeline told him, she did care.

From that night forward, Evangeline Duff wrapped her entire being in Archie's gentle and complete love. As a woman, she had waited all her life to hear these words. And now, she felt ready. Mature in Christ, confident in ministry, and happy in life, Archie's love was a marvelous bonus to her delightfully full life in Christ.

Yes, Evangeline cared.

CHAPTER SEVEN

Two Become One

*B*efore breakfast the next morning, in typical English fashion, Archie approached Evangeline's father, Reverend Walter Duff, and requested his daughter's hand in marriage. The prospect of such a fine son-in-law delighted the older Irishman, and the twinkle in his eyes let Evangeline know what had transpired—even before Archie explained.

Certain of their love, Archie and Evangeline made immediate plans for a wedding. Three weeks later, on January 28, 1936, they were married. Though they planned a church wedding, the sudden illness of their pastor forced them to change plans.

Dr. Crouser had known the McNeill family since 1915. He was part of the committee that invited Dr. John McNeill to the Church of the Open Door in Los Angeles. Though too ill to leave his home, he conducted the McNeill wedding—a small private ceremony—in his living room, assisted by Evangeline's father.

In 1936, with the Great Depression at its height, Archie and Evangeline had no pictures and few gifts to mark their wedding ceremony; but the depressed economy had little effect on their celebration. Evangeline's father had never seen a more radiant bride.

She wore an oyster white suit, carefully tailored and fitting her slim figure beautifully. Evangeline's mother, Mathilda, and sister Helen spared no effort in decorating Helen's home and garden with the flowers they so dearly loved. When the ceremony ended, the family celebrated with friends, food, and music at Helen's home.

Archie was beside himself with happiness. At last, the beautiful redhead he so admired ten years ago had chosen him. She had made his happiness even more complete by the deep and committed love she expressed in the note she wrote to him on the morning of their wedding. He would always treasure the message:

"My own dear Archie,

"This will probably be the last 'love note' you will receive from me before we are married. How happy I am dear, and how I love you. I admire your outstanding Christian qualities and on the other side your tender, loving spirit, and understanding ways. You have already made me so happy and I know the days to come will be 'Pleasant Paths.' I know we shall face difficulties and troubles but together it shall be easier.

"The lovely fellowship and prayer we had together last night was something I shall never forget. Oh you are so dear to me…how proud I shall be to be called by your name this afternoon."

The new couple had little time for a honeymoon. Archie withdrew from BIOLA and the bride and groom became a new evangelistic team. At first, they traveled with Evangeline's brother Walter. Together, Walter and Evangeline helped Archie develop his preaching skills. He and Walter took turns giving the evening message. Always ready to encourage and polish, Evangeline freely shared her own preaching experiences with her new husband.

Eventually, Evangeline and Archie held meetings without Walter—using music as their drawing card. His rich baritone voice, complemented by Evangeline's skill on the classical harp, piano, and vibraharp, made a strong impression on their audience. She added variety by accompanying herself as she sang the great hymns of the faith. They billed their work as "musicals," and Archie concluded every service with an evangelistic message.

In January 1937, Evangeline's father began publishing the *Monthly Evangel*, a magazine designed to publicize and support the growing number of evangelistic teams he sent out. He titled his organization, The American Christian Workers Union, after its Irish predecessor. Evangeline and Archie became one of his many teams. At this time, Evangeline wrote to Archie's mother, now widowed and living in Edinburgh, Scotland:

"You asked about the work which we are planning to do…Through the Northwest there is much need in rural communities and small villages for the preaching of the gospel. Even in northern California, we have found many, many places where there is not a service of any kind where one might hear a gospel message. It is to these needy fields we plan to go."

Archie and Evangeline purchased an old trailer and traveled from town to town. Evangeline, experienced in the work and with many helpful contacts, organized their schedules and managed the finances. In spite of the raging Depression, these small rural communities provided generous support. Though the offering frequently consisted entirely of small change, between God's provision and Evangeline's careful management, it was always enough.

Much to Evangeline's delight, Archie blossomed in his new ministry. He grew to become a wonderful "people person," a great song leader, and a dynamic preacher. In Stockton, California, only months after launching out on their own, a local pastor told Archie, "Young man, that was a great message and I believe you have a great future if you will remain faithful."

And remain faithful they did. In town after town, criss-crossing the western United States, the newlyweds brought many to Christ.

Evangeline loved to send and receive mail. Through her correspondence, she developed a strong and loving relationship with Archie's mother. In one letter she wrote:

"Last night, Archie gave a most searching message. Then on the other hand, he has a free and easy manner, which dispels all prejudice. Our musicals have been quite successful and we seem to be made for each other—that is—in our work, we agree perfectly."

<hr />

That winter, after a long series of appeals from Archie's Scottish family (many had not yet met Evangeline), the newlyweds planned a trip to Europe—a homecoming of sorts. Evangeline's father, and her brothers Haldane and Walter, (along with his wife Edith) would accompany them on the voyage. Evangeline and Archie planned to visit his family in England and Scotland and then spend time in the British Isles holding evangelistic meetings. The Duffs would visit relatives in Ireland.

Evangeline had great difficulty planning the trip. Ship after ship was too full to accommodate the large party. Finally, with reservations made, Evangeline and Archie left their beloved trailer with Helen (who had moved to Oregon), and started out across country by car to New York. Evangeline had given Helen instructions to sell the trailer for them, hoping that funds from the sale would clear the newlyweds of any outstanding debt and provide a fresh start when they returned from Europe.

On May 20, 1937, sailing aboard the Cunard White Star liner, *Berengaria*, they departed for Europe.

As soon as Evangeline and Archie left, Helen set out to find a buyer for the little trailer. A couple soon agreed to buy it, and Helen gave them the title in exchange for their check.

But when the couple went to register the trailer, they discovered that Helen did not have the legal power of attorney needed to complete the sale.

Evangeline and Archie were on board ship somewhere in the mid-Atlantic and could not be reached. They had borrowed money to buy the trailer and with the loan repayment date approaching quickly, Helen was frantic.

Suddenly the bank demanded payment in full. On the day payment became past due, the bank repossessed the trailer, sold it to Helen's buyers and kept the full amount of the sale. This left Helen with the job of explaining the bungle to Archie and Evangeline. Heartsick about the mistake, she took pen in hand:

"I can't help feeling it was my fault, yet I was so helpless. The bank would talk to no one nor make any terms. I surely believe that someone saw a chance to make some money for themselves and did so."

Offering to sell her only car to pay back the loss, Helen closed the letter, "I love you and Archie so much. In my lifetime, I'll find some way of making it up."

⸻

This disappointing news greeted Archie and Evangeline as soon as they reached Europe. Though they wouldn't consider Helen giving up her car, they wondered what to do next. The little trailer had been their sole investment toward the cost of starting over. $400 meant a great deal to Archie and Evangeline. Choosing to ignore their grief, they turned instead toward the opportunities before them.

Archie hoped for effective, life-changing ministry.

His father, the Scottish evangelist John McNeill had served as one of the most famous preachers of his century. He had pastored churches in Edinburgh, Regents Square, London, Liverpool, Toronto, Denver, Alabama, New York and Los Angeles. In every church, his congregations experienced enormous growth.

Even more important than his pastoral success, John McNeill left a legacy as an evangelist. Having worked with D.L. Moody, and Charles Spurgeon for more that 16 years, John McNeill frequently drew open-air crowds of more than 10,000 people.

Like Evangeline's father, Walter Duff Sr., John McNeill played an integral part in the extraordinary revival that swept the British Isles at the beginning of the twentieth century.

His powerful voice, dramatic flair, and delightful sense of humor combined with an almost supernatural understanding of the persons and truths of the Bible, made the elder McNeill extremely popular in both religious and popular circles. He had been active in preaching and evangelism throughout his later years, preaching his last sermon only two weeks before his death in 1933, at the age of 79. So great was his influence that three memorial services had been held in his honor—in London, Edinburgh and Glasgow.

Only 30 years after that great revival, the religious climate of western Europe had grown cold. The devastation of the First World War combined with the ensuing economic prosperity and sudden worldwide depression served to distract most of Europe from her earlier commitment.

In only one generation, the British Isles had fallen from faith.

This was the climate that greeted Archie and Evangeline. Yes, they planned to renew acquaintances from their youth. Yes, they would visit their families. But they would also hold evangelistic meetings. With God's favor, they hoped that John McNeill's popularity would translate into invitations for Archie and Evangeline.

Most importantly, the young couple hoped to return the hearts of their countrymen to God.

They enjoyed a delightful spring together. Traveling by rail, they went sight-seeing, visited relatives and, as always, held whatever meetings could be arranged. Archie had many family connections. His father's first wife had four children before dying suddenly in 1891. John McNeill had remarried in 1898, to Margaret Lee Millar, who gave him six more children. Archie was the youngest son of John and Margaret. Remarkably, Margaret had helped the children become a happy, committed family. Archie enjoyed spending time with his many siblings.

Archie had grown to resemble his father, John McNeill, in facial features and stature, although the son was a good deal taller than the father. Once in Europe, Archie grew a full beard, as his father had.

Archie's older brother, Cam, put him in his place. "You are not Father, Archie, and no amount of looking like him, will make you into the great John McNeill."

The beard came off.

While many churches opened their doors to Archie and Evangeline, the people did not respond either financially or spiritually. Dependent on the generosity of their audiences, the young McNeills found it difficult to make ends meet—even while staying with relatives. European audiences were hugely distracted by the political and social events surrounding them. Food and goods were scarce. Poverty was common.

The screaming Fuehrer of Germany had the full attention of everyone in Europe. He openly defied England and her beloved Prime Minister Chamberlain. Hitler stood with his toes on the line of democracy and dared Europe to stop him. Desperate to maintain peace, Chamberlain backed down from every challenge the German leader made. Though hundreds of miles apart, the two leaders exchanged veiled threats and appeasements via the press and the British Broadcasting Company.

With the threat of another war hanging over every political exchange, few paused to consider the young American preacher's message.

During that same spring, on another continent, the American Christian Workers Union continued to grow. Evangeline's mother Mathilda and her sister, Helen Baugh moved into an old farm in Wonder, Oregon. Their large home became the Union headquarters. An older couple served as caretakers for the farm, leaving Helen and Mrs. Duff free to organize and host the evangelistic teams who came and went. As always, Helen organized a large network of prayer support for the Union.

In 1937 the world stood on the brink. There appeared to be only two camps: Those who believed war was inevitable and those desperate to deny the political danger boiling in Europe and Japan. Noisy isolationists sprang up in the United States. Newspapers carried editorials and articles espousing the wisdom of minding one's own business.

But those opinions did not fool one petite, brown-eyed, gray-haired Oregon grandmother. She watched Hitler come to power in 1934. She heard him declare the end to the Versailles Treaty in 1935. She watched him re-arm and re-militarize Germany. And she watched as he took the Rhineland in 1936. She'd heard and understood the English commitment to "non-intervention."

But none of these facts alarmed her as much as the news from the Christian press. Even before secular periodicals published the facts, Mrs. Mathilda Hamilton Duff sensed what was about to unfold.

Under Hitler the church in Germany suffered intense persecution, beginning with regulations to support the NAZI agenda from the pulpit. Next, knowing that a church without funds could not survive, Hitler forbade taking offerings. Finally, he enforced regulations to proclaim a gospel foreign to the Bible (that Jesus Himself was not Jewish). In the end, Hitler forcibly closed the Christian churches of Germany.

But Hitler had not anticipated the tenacity of God's people. Before any other voice of resistance rose in Germany, believers spoke out. Hitler singled them out for destruction. Resistant pastors were arrested, beaten and imprisoned. Parishioners were jailed. Persecution of the Jews aroused the conscience of those who belonged to Jesus. As the only group who raised themselves against the Nazi regime, Christians branded themselves to join the persecuted.

The Church in the United States heard their cry. Mathilda Duff heard it.

As early as 1936, dire predictions filled the Christian press. One publication quoted a German pastor, "Soon, within not more than 10 or 20 years, you Americans will be called upon to face what we are going through."

The Jewish persecution alarmed Mathilda. The *Christian Century* published the resignation of James G. McDonald, "High Commissioner for the Refugees Coming From Germany." His letter appealed to the League of Nations for intervention in the matter of Jewish persecution in Germany, which he said, "…now makes it difficult for these (Jews) to sustain life." In his opinion, the problem had grown in gravity and complexity until it had become a danger to international peace. Intervention, he felt, was desperately needed.

Mathilda Duff knew her Bible. She understood Jewish persecution. As the temperature of world politics increased, her prayer for the safety of her husband and children in Europe became more fervent.

She was not silent about her fear. "Please consider cutting short your trip," she wrote to Evangeline. "The persecution of the Jews in Germany mounts. I am afraid that we are in for a very dangerous war. Though I don't want to shortchange your work of the Lord, I long for you all to come home."

Father, Haldane, Walter, and Edith found conditions in Ireland to be as difficult for the gospel as for the McNeills in England. The Duffs agreed to separate, doing their best to cover more territory. But both the crowds and offerings were small. Having no other way to support their work, they too wondered what the Lord had in mind.

Then Haldane Duff accepted a speaking engagement in Berlin. Though he understood the danger, he could not ignore the opportunity. He knew of no other place on earth more desperately in need of the Gospel. After some discussion among the family, Haldane agreed to go.

Mathilda wrote frequently to her family. It was no secret that she badly missed them all. She kept track of their comings and goings. They corresponded too—though largely through postcards. When she could, Evangeline was careful to write long descriptions of their trips and meetings. She knew how lonesome her mother was. And, more than the others, Evangeline sensed her mother's mounting anxiety about their safety. Though Evangeline's news came regularly, it barely stifled Mathilda's growing anxiety. Then Mathilda sensed something terribly wrong. She had not heard from Haldane. No one else wrote of him either.

Neither the Irish Duffs, nor the Scottish McNeills knew what had happened. Suddenly Haldane cut off communication. They increased their prayer on his behalf.

When the German borders closed, they wondered how they would ever find him.

Just as they began official search proceedings, they received a wire from Haldane requesting money. Walter Duff smiled as he read the wire. *Every family expects the youngest to wire for money,* he thought. *Haldane must be safe.*

When he returned to Ireland, Haldane's story frightened them more than his disappearance. In Berlin he had been arrested and detained as a spy. Though his American citizenship protected him, he was changed by the experience. This terrifying episode, combined with Mathilda's frequent appeals to return home, convinced the Duffs to return to the United States.

Just one month later, in late November, 1937 Archie and Evangeline followed them. The young McNeills crossed the Atlantic for the last time. With what little savings they had left, they purchased a used car in New York City. Gradually, holding meetings along the way, they worked their way back to the West Coast.

CHAPTER EIGHT

Home Again

By Christmas 1937 all the Duff children had returned to Oregon. Happiest of all was the diminutive grandmother who had prayed her children safely home. Before the holiday meal she prayed. "I praise you Lord for your protection. Praise your wonderful name. You have been so faithful. How good to have a father in heaven who loves us and provides for us and takes care of all our problems."

When the new year dawned, Archie and Evangeline still faced one insurmountable dilemma. With no trailer, and no money, they could not travel along the coast as they had. So they focused on villages near Wonder, Oregon, seizing whatever opportunity they could. By spring Archie and Evangeline had a new concern; they were expecting a baby.

Needing to provide for his new family, Archie sought a more permanent position than that of itinerant evangelist. They began to look for a pastorate.

Two different congregations expressed a serious interest in Archie's ministry, both in Portland, Oregon. One was a large successful church with a lovely manse. The other was a church so rundown that the board had nearly decided to disband rather than fill the pulpit. Archie and Evangeline committed the question to prayer. Together they decided to let the Lord decide. They would accept the first response they received. In August, their letter of acceptance came from the board of Calvary Presbyterian Church.

The letter, dated August 29, 1938, stated, "This presentation (of Archie's candidacy to the congregation) I am glad to report, was accepted at said meeting without a dissenting vote of any kind." Less than twenty-four hours later the other church also urged Archie to accept their pastorate.

Archie and Evangeline began their work at Calvary Presbyterian on September 1, 1938, renting a tiny, three-room apartment just blocks from the church. Though it was small, and had no windows, Evangeline delighted in her first opportunity to make a real home. She settled in with joy.

Located in an area of town bordering on "Goose Hollow," the neighborhood near Calvary Presbyterian was considered downtown, in an age of migration away from the city. A great variety of people lived in the neighborhood, including both the very poor and the very wealthy.

From Archie's first day in the pulpit, it was clear to him that there was very little life left in either the building or the dwindling congregation of less than one hundred members. With few funds, the older church building had fallen into serious disrepair.

Evangeline and Archie began immediately to plan their approach. From the first day they bathed their work with prayer. Both had a longstanding concern for unsaved youth in each community they touched. They agreed that only young people could bring life and vitality to Calvary's older congregation.

The Goose Hollow area of Portland's west side teamed with young people. Heavy drinking and Saturday night carousing made family life miserable for many of the teens. Many children knew only one parent—divorce was rampant. These young people would not be an easy audience.

Together, Archie and Evangeline found satisfaction in planning ways to reach the young adults living in their neighborhood. They held special meetings for the teens. They scheduled street parades, and street witnessing. They worked. They prayed. And God answered. In a short time, their congregation began to include a vital group of young persons.

Archie's preaching also attracted a group of young-married couples searching for a church home. Word quickly circulated that something exciting was happening at Calvary Presbyterian. Sunday evening services swelled to accommodate those of other congregations who came to hear the good preaching of the young Scottish pastor.

The congregation continued to grow. But God had plans for Evangeline and Archie to grow as well. During their time at Calvary Presbyterian, a retired missionary from the Christian and Missionary Alliance church lived in Portland. Though nearly 90 and completely blind, Mrs. Harding began a ministry to Portland area pastors.

Each Wednesday, she invited them to her home where she challenged them with difficult, intellectual Bible work. "Ministers," she said lovingly, "are a mentally lazy lot. And God cannot use a lazy mind. We must work our mind as we work our body in order to keep it fit for the Master."

To illustrate her point, Mrs. Harding would interrupt her teaching with long multi-step math problems—demanding her listeners solve them without pencil and paper. She stumped the pastors. Before any could answer, the elderly blind woman had the answer herself. She did not demand anything of them that she could not do herself. Archie and Evangeline never missed an opportunity to be with Mrs. Harding.

She challenged them to memorize scripture, and under her teaching the McNeill's both strove to successfully memorize large portions of scripture. The work of an old, handicapped woman influenced their ministry for life.

Archie and Evangeline experienced other joys in Portland. On October 5, 1938, Isabelle Duff McNeill was born. Archie and Evangeline, both in their mid-thirties, had never experienced anything so wonderful. Yes, married life satisfied them both. But to Archie, this charming, wonderful, helpless, baby girl was his greatest gift.

Evangeline thought that perhaps Archie was the most devoted father ever to walk the earth. Isabelle accompanied her parents on every outing. She went along to services, speaking engagements, and ministry trips. The youth of Calvary Presbyterian adopted Isabelle as well, happily including her whenever she came along.

Archie and Evangeline were not satisfied with simply bringing the young persons in their community to church. They wanted more. They wanted genuine conversions. And still more. They wanted disciples. And more. They wanted to teach the young people to take on the ministry. To make it their own.

For this reason, Archie often took a team of committed young people to visit any number of locations—jails, hospitals, and unwed-mothers' homes—anywhere he felt the gospel was needed. He prepared them for ministry by teaching them to share their faith, and by showing them the importance of bathing their ministry efforts in prayer.

Evangeline and Archie took their work very seriously. Archie was not afraid to march down the aisle of the local theatre to retrieve members of his youthful congregation when movies of questionable content were shown. He would run through neighborhoods chasing boys who avoided his fatherly devotion. But, rather than drive the teenagers away, his devotion and strictness drew them in. Their number grew.

Unlike other pastors in Portland, Archie kept his home open at all hours. Whether to discuss romantic disappointments or to talk of weighty spiritual matters, Archie was always available. Through his front doors flowed an endless line of young persons needing pastoral attention.

Archie and Evangeline also believed that teenagers needed time together, for recreation, as well as relationships. For this reason, Archie punctuated his time at Calvary Presbyterian with swimming trips to "Romer's Rest" on the Tualatin River, picnics on Lake Oswego, and camping trips to Driftwood Auto Court in the tiny village of Cannon Beach, along the Oregon coast.

Archie understood the distractions in the young people's busy lives. So, he and Evangeline came up with another innovative idea. They took the young people camping for a week. While away, the teens would spend time in recreation together—and have ample opportunity for intensive bible teaching.

The group went to many locations; but by far the most successful was the Driftwood Auto Park at Cannon Beach, Oregon where they brought as many as forty teens at a time. They rented a truck to carry their gear, and persuaded members of their congregation to help with the cooking and chaperoning. After borrowing a trailer for themselves and their daughter, they headed for the coast.

The teens reveled in the attention. They set up their own tents, each having it's own name: the "Dew-Drop Inn," the "Just Squeeze Inn," the "Brush Inn" and of course, the McNeill's own borrowed trailer was christened the "Seldom Inn."

Even in Depression days, a week of camping was a bargain. Food, transportation, park rental, plus incidentals cost just $4. Though conditions were rough, the Goose Hollow kids loved it. They ate together on long plank tables, walked the beach, rode bicycles, and occasionally rode horses from the nearby stable. Every day, Archie and Evangeline provided morning Bible studies and evening devotions.

Having taught horseback riding in California, Archie loved horses. He loved to take the children on long horse rides beside the surf. Evangeline loved the beach as well. She grew to love the sand, the wind, the ever-changing sky and the enormous, endless sea.

Of course Isabelle went along on every trip, drawing endless attention from the girls and enjoying the boys' roughhousing.

Along with the play, the sand castles, the campfires and song, the teens loved the teaching. Archie delivered gentle sermons full of love—the kind of teaching that lasts a lifetime.

While lives were changing on the beach, the world was also changing. The United States entered the Second World War. Overwhelmed by the desire to speak to the young soldiers going overseas, Archie began going to the Portland Serviceman's Center, where he told them about their need for Jesus. Gently, fervently, he spoke to lonely, frightened servicemen about the Captain of the Lord's Army.

Like his father before him, Archie felt the urgent spiritual need of these young soldiers. During World War I, John McNeill left an American pastorate to return to Scotland, where he joined the British Military as a chaplain. John McNeill brought many young soldiers to Christ. As the days of World War II progressed, Archie understood for the first time, the seriousness that surrounded his father during the war years.

Archie knew that many of these men would never return.

Initially a cooperative venture of local Portland churches, the Serviceman's Center also provided a wonderful opportunity for the people in Archie's congregation to practice their evangelistic skills. Frequently they accompanied Archie to the Serviceman's Center. An evangelist at heart, Archie was very successful at bringing these military men to Christ. His imposing stature somehow took away their picture of Jesus being only for the impotent and weak-kneed.

As the war dragged on, after long days at work, Archie went to the Serviceman's Center. Evangeline hosted dinners for an endless line of young soldiers. Her hospitality provided a family connection for young men, often away from home for the first time. Between her loving concern, and his persuasive witness, many soldiers left for war ready to meet eternity.

In the late spring of 1940, Evangeline and Archie happily discovered that they were expecting another baby. Because of the great joy Isabelle brought to their lives, they could hardly wait for another child.

The pregnancy appeared to progress normally until one Friday morning in early October. Evangeline, who had just finished her weekly washing and begun picking up in the kitchen, quickly realized that something was wrong. She called Archie, who took her to the hospital to meet their doctor. The news was not good. Twenty-five weeks into the pregnancy, her amniotic sac had broken. If born at this stage of development, the baby had little chance of survival. Their only hope was to hold off labor and delivery.

Her doctor admitted Evangeline to the hospital and ordered complete bed rest. No matter how difficult Evangeline found lying still, she became a model patient. She would do whatever was necessary to give her baby a fighting chance.

Happily, labor did not occur. One week later, with the baby doing well, and Evangeline's condition stabilized, she was discharged from the hospital with strict orders to continue resting as much as possible.

Then on October 29, Evangeline woke with a fever. After a day of complete bed rest, the fever continued. At Archie's urging, she called the doctor. Soon after labor began. Again they went to the hospital.

Though the medical staff tried to stop the labor, the newest McNeill baby was born at 6:55 A.M. the next morning. Archie stayed with Evangeline during the delivery. With gratitude for the baby's life, they named him James Duff McNeill.

But the new baby was not well. At 29 weeks gestation, he weighed only 3 lbs. 5 oz. Though Archie and Evangeline began to pray, the baby lived only two hours and 22 minutes.

Though short, the baby's life touched his parents deeply. Archie was heartbroken. Evangeline was crushed.

When she was able, Evangeline came home to her tiny apartment. Friends cared for Isabelle as Archie went back to work. Left in the little apartment by herself, Evangeline grieved alone. The delivery had seriously affected her heath. Anemic and weak, doctors worked to bolster her blood.

But Evangeline was weak of spirit as well. The tiny congregation did what they could. They cooked meals. They cleaned. They babysat. But they could not fight the long and lonely battle that loomed in Evangeline's spirit.

Hers was a battle of grief—a battle of trust.

As the winter of 1941 came to a close, the darkness lifted. As Jacob of old, Evangeline had struggled with God. She too, came away limping.

In spite of their grief, Archie's pastorate at Calvary Presbyterian continued with obvious success. His hard work and determination, combined with his most unusual faith and creativity brought an increase in both attendance and giving. These results delighted the Church Board of Elders.

In the second winter of his pastorate, Archie realized that the outside of the old, ornate building needed extensive renovation. The board wanted to raise funds in the old-fashioned way, with fund drives and appeals from the pulpit. Instead Archie sent a letter to his congregation. "Rather than engage in lengthy and offensive fund raising," he explained, "we will instead meet for prayer about the matter on Wednesday evening. Certainly our Father knows about our need, and He can supply our need as well."

They raised the funds without another word. Word of Archie's unusual approach eventually reached the pages of the Portland daily newspaper.

Though Archie accepted the Calvary pastorate without being officially ordained in the Presbyterian Church, the search committee's concerns, openly expressed, continued to trouble him. Was he licensed? Where had he been educated?

As the congregation grew to love and respect the work of their dedicated new pastor, they put these former questions aside. But Archie never did.

Even as he pastored Calvary Presbyterian and worked at the Serviceman's Center, he sought and received his official ordination on April 30, 1943.

In spite of Archie's hard work, the Second World War took its toll on the congregation. Eventually, nearly every able-bodied young man left Portland to join the military. Attendance dwindled. At the same time, the numbers of those who were too young to fight grew. These often badly behaved young people tried the patience of the elders and board members.

At the same time church friction increased, the Serviceman's Center board of directors noticed Archie's deep commitment to their ministry. The center had continued to grow, and their director needed additional help. It was only natural for the board to invite Archie to join them as the new associate director.

The opportunity forced Archie to a difficult decision. Many of the young men who passed through the center would have no other opportunity to make a decision for Christ—a serious issue that weighed heavily on Archie. Yet, he was deeply committed to the ministry of Calvary Presbyterian. He had just celebrated his ordination. It was not so much a matter of which position to choose, as it was a matter of which position to relinquish. Such a decision would certainly change the course of his life.

Rev. Archie McNeill in 1951

Evangeline Duff (McNeill) with concert harp in 1920s

The Duff Family in International Falls, Minnesota, after the birth of baby Haldane. From left, first row: Walter Sr., Haldane. Second row: Olive, Walter Jr., (Alexandria) Evangeline. Back row: Helen, Matilda.

Evangeline and sister Helen with a "motorhome" about 1918

Evangeline in 1930s

Archie and Evangeline, wedding photo, 1936

The old Bill Hotel, the original site of the Cannon Beach Conference Center, in the summer of 1945

The first Chapel of the Conference Center is on right, cabins on left

Evangeline and Archie, summer 1949

The first summer guests at the Conference Center, July 1945

Archie and Evangeline with daughter Heather (Isabelle) and
"Snooper," 1945

Archie with Evangeline at the piano, 1940s.

Sunset Highway Crash Fatal to Cannon Beach Man

This picture was taken by Pete White, Portland fireman, few minutes after Archie McNeill, Cannon Beach, was fatally injured in a collision between his car and truck on Sunset highway. McNeill, who was traveling west, may have been blinded by late afternoon sun. His body lies in the foreground. Trucker escaped with scratches.

2 Ordinances Before Council

GLADSTONE, Aug. 6 (Special)—Two ordinances, water supply and sewage disposal, and councilmanic elections were on the agenda of the city council Tuesday night.

An ordinance vacating Yale street between the school grounds and the new city park was passed at first reading. Another city law regarding negligent driving also was given approval on the insistence of Chief Clarence Moore.

A report of the state board of health cleared the city's auxiliary water supply, Mayor Walter Brunner reported. The auxiliary well was tapped into the city domestic water supply when the river-side well was unable to provide sufficient water for summer-time demands, he said.

Clerk Gene Good was authorized to inform the Portland Traction company to live up to its agreement to keep pavement repaired on Portland avenue, where PTC trolleys operate.

Action Delayed

Preliminary discussion of the pact with Oregon City for the latter city's sewage disposal plant was perfunctory, Brunner reported.

Rev. Archie McNeill, 46, owner and director of the Cannon Beach Bible Conference grounds, was fatally injured in a traffic accident on Sunset highway Tuesday afternoon. His car collided with a truck three miles east of Timber junction, just inside Tillamook county.

McNeill died a few minutes after he was removed from his smashed 1951 automobile. Alex Getz, 8054 S. E. 9th avenue, driver of the truck, was unhurt except for a scratch on the cheek, although his truck was turned on its side.

Getz told state police McNeill's car came toward him on the wrong side of the road. Officers said McNeill could have been blinded by the sun. He was going west when the accident occurred at 4:45 p. m.

Accident Blocks Traffic

McNeill was returning from Portland, where he had gone to get supplies for his establishment. The groceries with which he had filled his car were strewn on the highway. Traffic was blocked for a short time.

The body was taken to the Tillamook county morgue by Allen E. Lundberg, coroner.

Getz is a driver for Porter W. Yett construction company, which has a resurfacing job in the Quartz creek bridge section of the highway. His dump truck was empty.

McNeill was born in Scotland. He is survived by the widow, Evangeline, two daughters, Isabel, 14, and Helen Jean, about 3; his mother, Mrs. Margaret McNeill in St. Alden, England, a brother in South Africa; and a half-sister in Scotland and another in England.

Rev. Archie McNeill, director of Cannon Beach Bible conference grounds, was injured fatally in traffic accident Tuesday on Sunset highway.

Bid Call Near On Rogue Job

WASHINGTON, Aug. 6 (AP) The bureau of reclamation hopes to start rehabilitation work on the Savage Rapids dam near Grants Pass, Or., in the fall of 1953, the office of Senator Guy Cordon, Republican, Oregon, reported Wednesday.

Bids on the new gates for the Rogue river structure are expected to be called next month. Because of the steel involved these are considered the most likely source of possible delay.

Robert Parkman, the senator's administrative aide, told a reporter he had been advised that designs for the rehabilitated dam are expected to be complete by May 15, 1953, with contract letting planned for six weeks later.

Congress Votes $700,000

Actual work, however, won't get under way until late September or October, at the end of the summer's irrigation season. The bureau hopes to be able to complete the work prior to the 1954 irrigation year.

Congress appropriated $700,000 for the rehabilitation work.

Evangeline, late 1950s

Evangeline in the 1970s

CHAPTER NINE

A New Ministry

As with all important decisions, Archie and Evangeline gave the issue of the Serviceman's Center much attention and prayer. In May of 1943, Archie called a congregational meeting, and read his letter of resignation from the pulpit:

"It is now almost five years ago that your session asked me to supply the pulpit of Calvary Church, and I hardly realize that these years have passed so rapidly. They have been pleasant years for Mrs. McNeill and myself. There have been difficult places, but you have most wonderfully stood by me through them. We have learned to know each other's faults and failings, but as in a human family, these are often easily surmounted by our love for one another and overshadowing (that), our supreme love for Christ.

"I have prayed earnestly for each of you as you have faced perplexities and troubles. I know you have done the same for me. God has, on many occasions, marvelously answered and so, as we look at our church building today—so beautifully decorated, we feel He alone has all the glory. This is but one of His manifold blessings.

"One of my greatest joys since being here has been the fine group of young men whom God was pleased to send us.

Today they are scattered in many parts of the world, fighting for God and country. I pray for them. From time to time they have written me and urged me to do all in my power for the servicemen—to preach to them, to try to lead them to the Savior. For they realize all too well, a great many will never return.

"About six weeks ago, I was approached by the United Christian Serviceman's Center…I had been approached several times before, but had never considered it. Other calls had come from other churches from time to time likewise, but I was happy in my work at Calvary and felt this was my field. This particular day, God spoke to my heart about it, and it seemed I could not throw it off. I took it to God in prayer. He answered. Today, I feel that God has given me 'marching orders' and I simply asked that this meeting be called to tender my resignation as pastor of this dear church."

⁎

Though the McNeill's ended their leadership at Calvary Presbyterian, they continued to call it their church home. Having the continued support of old friends helped them transition to new work with the Serviceman's Center. And once again they had time to accept invitations to speak at area churches and events.

Archie became a favorite baccalaureate and graduation speaker. He spoke for civic events as well, including Rotary and Kiwanis. Weeklong crusades for both youths and adults often featured Archie McNeill who traveled as far as California to fulfill the many requests. At the same time, he continued to hold evangelistic services in local congregations. Many audiences in Oregon and Washington grew to love the great big preacher with the sweet face and Scottish accent.

During the McNeill's years at Calvary Presbyterian, Evangeline's sister Helen moved back to San Jose, California. There, she and her husband Elwood Baugh began a small ministry to Christian professional women. At first, they held small weekly meetings in local restaurants. The interest in her new group surprised Helen Duff Baugh.

She began to invite speakers from nearby communities. The group grew rapidly. Evangeline's father saw the ministry having widespread potential, and he began to encourage Helen to plant similar groups in other cities. A short time later, Evangeline and her father organized a similar women's group in Portland.

Both groups grew with surprising speed, eventually becoming the innocent beginning of the Christian Business and Professional Women's Council. The San Jose group soon took on the support of two young women who brought the gospel message to small villages via summer Bible camps or "After School Clubs."

Evangeline and Helen's groups gave birth to councils and missionaries in other cities. The McNeill home in Portland became the overnight stay for these young missionaries as they traveled between villages and the unofficial headquarters of this new organization. Evangeline converted an upstairs room into guest quarters. Archie found himself transporting the missionaries to and from the bus depot.

More than a hostess, Evangeline began visiting nearby locations to assist women in establishing their own groups. She helped the ladies plan, publicize and carry out their first meetings. Available to help in any way—cooking, serving, cleaning—Evangeline often served as the featured speaker as well.

During the remainder of the war, Archie and Evangeline worked endlessly—Archie at the Serviceman's Center, and Evangeline with the Clubs and Councils. A constant stream of young soldiers passed through the McNeill household. The board of the Serviceman's Center was delighted with Archie's work.

By early 1944, Americans began to dream of victory. The United States, with an astronomical investment of men and equipment bound for Europe, began to hope that the end would soon come.

Archie and Evangeline had more on their minds than the war in Europe, or even the Christian Women's Clubs and Councils. They had begun to dream about a new ministry. A new goal had sprung from Archie's evangelistic outreach.

As the featured speaker at many weeklong retreats, Archie was struck by the increased attention of his audiences. Unlike Sunday congregations, these were undistracted by responsibility, focused entirely on the speaker's presentation—responding quickly to the Word of God. There was a freedom for these audiences that Archie found new and wonderful.

In spite of this excitement, Archie experienced disappointment as well. Often at a weeklong conference, Archie watched many people make decisions for Christ. Unfortunately, after a week of teaching, Archie returned to Portland and the new Christians returned to life in these small towns with little support.

Archie felt his old love for young people spring up again. Together, he and Evangeline talked these things over with the Lord in prayer. Eventually, they began to wonder together: What if there was a place that offered weeklong conferences to young people? Could this provide a new way to reach young persons for Christ—to move them toward maturity and commitment for ministry in Christ?

The possibility excited them. The week they envisioned would be a holiday combined with Bible study, resulting in a definite time of growth. To meet these needs, they reasoned, the retreat should occur in a recreational area. Though it was only a dream, it was something they regularly prayed about. Gradually, they came to the consensus that the dream might be the leading of the Lord, and, wanting to cooperate, they began to look for a suitable location while they continued to pray.

In the spring of that year, as they traveled, they prayed for eyes to see God's arrangements. Though they frequently found beautiful property, they knew that buildings would be a prerequisite. Because of the war, serious restrictions were placed on all types of building materials. They simply had to have a building ready to go.

Evangeline and Archie had limited financial resources. How could an evangelist, and associate director of a Serviceman's Center even begin to consider the purchase of recreational property?

Evangeline's father, now nearly 70, continued to conduct evangelistic services across the United States. With her father away at a Denver, Colorado conference, Evangeline asked her mother, Mathilda, to join them for a few days' holiday at Cannon Beach. Since their days of beach camping with the youth of Calvary Presbyterian, the McNeill's considered Cannon Beach a favorite "get-away." Mathilda, delighted, joined Archie and Evangeline and Isabelle as they headed for the beach.

One morning, Evangeline took a walk from their campground into the tiny village of Cannon Beach. As she crossed the bridge over Elk Creek, she was struck by the incredible beauty of the old Cannon Beach Hotel, a large log building of two stories, covered with climbing vines.

The grass in the unkempt grounds had been taken over by wildflowers, and Evangeline found the view so stunning that she caught her breath. Both the flowers and the vines were in full bloom. *How lovely*, she thought. Continuing on her way, a thought struck her, *Could this be it? Is this the property we are praying for?*

Turning into the driveway, she walked through knee-high grass. The hotel was closed—and had been for a long time. The building had fallen into serious disrepair. Still, she edged her way carefully across the old porch and peered into the dirty, paned windows.

Her heart beat faster as she wandered from window to window straining to see the dimensions of the dark rooms inside. Certain this was a wonderful discovery. Evangeline hurried away to find Archie.

When he first glimpsed Evangeline hurrying toward him, her red hair glistened in the sun, and her form was so beautiful he couldn't help but admire his wife as she came closer. Then he became alarmed. She had only just left for town. What brought her back so soon? Her face was flushed. In her hurry, she was out of breath. Still some distance away, she caught his eyes and flashed a radiant smile.

Beckoning, she called, "Come with me Archie—I've found something wonderful." Setting down his coffee, he went to meet her.

Together they walked the grounds of the old hotel. The property possessed many of the qualities they had prayed for. "Let's find a real estate man," Archie suggested. "Certainly he will know if this property is available."

It turned out that there was only one realtor in Cannon Beach. Yes, he knew about the property. No, it was definitely not for sale. Yes, he knew the owner. In fact, the only realtor in town, George Frisbee, also happened to own the old "Cannon Beach Hotel."

As Mr. Frisbee walked Archie and Evangeline from his office to the hotel, he relayed the long and illustrious history of the old building. Around the turn of the century loggers had made the first attempt to tow a cigar raft, made of logs, across the bar of the Columbia River. The attempt ended in disaster as the raft broke up in heavy seas and logs drifted south, eventually landing on the sand at Cannon Beach.

Mr. George Bill, a Cannon Beach resident, recovered the derelict logs and used them along with other hand-hewn lumber to build the old building. He managed the hotel during the days of stagecoach travel between Astoria and Tillamook.

In those days, the stage traveled south along the beach following the rugged terrain of an old Indian Trail. In areas where the path was too narrow for more than a single coach, the driver often had to stop and give a bellow that echoed from nearby rock cliffs. If he heard no response, he knew the road was clear.

There was no bridge over Elk Creek in those days. In order to cross, a wagon had to stop and wait for a falling tide. Sometimes the water was deeper than anticipated, and came up over the seats of the wagon drenching passengers, baggage and supplies.

The route around the narrow ledge at Hug Point required the stage and passengers to wait in Cannon Beach for another low tide before proceeding south. The Bill's Hotel provided the perfect stopping place. Here the passengers enjoyed a good meal and a long rest before they continued their journey.

The hotel was sold in 1913 to Edna Osborne, who changed the name to the Cannon Beach Hotel, continuing its successful operation. She, along with her parents, developed the inn's reputation for extraordinary dining. Under her management, the hotel was visited by some of Oregon's finest families along with President Woodrow Wilson and William Jennings Bryan.

Edna eventually married George Frisbee, and together they ran the hotel for the next few years. During the First World War however, the Coast Guard needed the building, housing more than one hundred men there.

Mr. Frisbee reported that since the first war, the hotel had not been used or maintained. No, it was not for sale, he repeated. But, should he and Edna decide to sell in the future, they would only consider a cash offer.

Disappointed, Evangeline and Archie toured the old log building anyway. Approaching the front entrance from the west they crossed a wide covered porch to face a heavy wooden door held closed by a huge ship's lock. Tiny windowpanes, nearly covered by vines and profuse shrubbery, framed the door.

Inside, they discovered a 30-by-50 foot lounge, punctuated at its southwest end by a massive fireplace of smooth river rock.

With a firebox 42 inches wide and 3 feet high, the stones extended to the ceiling. The fireplace dominated the room, which served as both a dining area and a lounge. In the opposite corner, stood an attached "lean to" kitchen for the preparation of meals.

The building's logs were not uniform in size, nor had they been peeled before they were notched and set in place. The walls, with no paint or plaster, provided a dark envelope surrounding the great room. At the northern end, a narrow staircase led to a small landing then turned and proceeded to the second floor.

Upstairs, a narrow hallway ran the length of the center of the building. Here, Archie and Evangeline found 10 large bedrooms, five with a view of the sea, and five overlooking the beautiful coastal mountains. At the end of the hall were rustic communal bathroom facilities. The single stone fireplace downstairs heated the entire building.

Returning downstairs to the main room, Mr. Frisbee asked Archie and Evangeline about their plans for the old rundown building. With great excitement, Archie explained his dream of a youth camp and conference center. Mr. Frisbee listened attentively, and though he seemed pleased with the thought of using the building for this purpose, he remained adamant. He would only consider a cash offer.

Graciously, the realtor and pastor parted company. Mr. Frisbee headed for his office in the village, while Archie and Evangeline returned to the campground.

"The place is perfect," Evangeline said. "It has a great location, good size, such potential—well not truly perfect—but, we have the vision, the energy, the dream. It could be perfect…" But for one insurmountable problem. Cash.

Together, Archie and Evangeline schemed. How could they buy the property? Through the rest of their beach vacation, they continued to return to the old hotel. Sometimes they met Mr. Frisbee there. While he continued to be gracious, he would not waver in his demand for a cash sale. Many times they returned alone—to plan, to dream, to pray—but no answer came to them. When their vacation ended, with some sadness, they returned to their city home.

In Portland, Archie and Evangeline continued to make the Cannon Beach site the subject of much prayer. After several weeks, they made arrangements to meet Mr. Frisbee at the hotel one last time.

On an unusually beautiful fall day Archie and Evangeline headed toward the coast, enjoying the cool air and brilliant fall dress of the vine maple. Both enjoyed a lightness of heart that could not be explained by the weather. Could this be the day that they would make the old hotel their own?

Once again Mr. Frisbee let them in through the grand old door. Again they toured the upstairs bedrooms. At last the three of them stood chatting by the fireplace. Mr. Frisbee had not changed his mind. He wanted cash—more cash than any preacher could readily obtain during war years. As they visited, Evangeline noticed a pickup truck turn into the driveway. Excusing himself, Mr. Frisbee said, "This man also wants to purchase the property." Disappointed, Evangeline watched him head out to greet the visitor.

Archie and Evangeline knew that only prayer would break their impasse with Mr. Frisbee. Together, they knelt on the old fireplace hearth. Archie began, "Lord, we do not want this property for our own use. We only want it for Thy Glory. We cannot purchase it for cash," Archie paused. "But Lord, you told us that 'The king's heart is in the hand of the Lord, as rivers of water; He turneth it whithersoever He will.' Now Lord, if you want us to have it, it is nothing for you to change Mr. Frisbee's heart."

When Mr. Frisbee returned, he said nothing of what had transpired on the driveway. "I will see you in Portland one of these days," he said during an awkward good-bye. So without any real answers, Archie and Evangeline made the long and silent trip back to Portland.

In Portland, the McNeills immediately returned to busy lives. They had scheduled a series of citywide meetings further east, on the Columbia River, near The Dalles, Oregon. Still disappointed about the old hotel, they drove to The Dalles where Archie and Evangeline stayed with friends.

One warm afternoon, their host, Mrs. Brickwedell, answered the phone to find a Mr. Frisbee on the line from Cannon Beach. He had traced Archie and Evangeline all the way to The Dalles in order to offer them the property exactly according to the terms they had offered.

That night in the Brickwedell home, the two couples enjoyed a great celebration. Only God could have accomplished such a miracle. Their revelry was full of joy, of praise, and of immense gratitude.

When they finally met to sign the real estate contract, Mr. Frisbee reminded them of their last meeting at the old hotel. He asked, "Did you ever wonder what happened when I went outside? The man in the truck handed me payment in full for the price of the property. I took the payment, but somehow—I don't know how to explain this—I didn't want the money. I wanted you folks to have the property. So, I told him, 'I'm sorry, the property has just been sold.'"

On September 23, 1944, the young McNeills signed a contract for the purchase of seven acres, a hotel building, and several outbuildings located in the tiny village of Cannon Beach, Oregon. Archie and Evangeline viewed that day as more than just an opportunity to sign real estate papers. For them, Mr. Frisbee's little story confirmed their new 'marching orders' from God. Buying the hotel on contract provided tangible evidence that God had indeed led them into a new ministry.

As the end of the war in Europe and the Pacific approached, Archie realized that the flow of young soldiers into Portland would end. The Serviceman's Center would close and Archie would be free to follow this new lead. They had no doubt. The conference center was God's new task, His new purpose for the two of them. As they signed the contract,

Archie and Evangeline, with all their heart and all their worldly goods, made a commitment to pursue God's new direction.

They believed God would continue to lead. He would accomplish the rest of their task. No worry about the future could ever take away the peace they felt in their heart. God had shown His divine direction. He had set His perfect stamp of provision on the dream they dared to dream.

CHAPTER TEN

The First Summer

❧

*A*fter much thought, Archie and Evangeline named their
new baby the Cannon Beach Bible Conference, taking
possession of the property in December. No dreary Oregon
winter could dampen their enthusiasm for the project. The
Duffs and McNeills frequently gathered down at the beach to
clean up the old hotel. With so much to do—furnishings to
find, a kitchen to establish, weeds to remove, and flowers to
plant—they needed every able body they could enlist.

Slowly the old hotel took on a new look. They made the
four small cabins into family guest rooms. They turned the
old officer's quarters ("The Annex") into deluxe accommodations—after all the rooms had sinks! The log hotel had 10
rooms upstairs, with bathrooms located at the end of the
hallway. They would use the main floor of the log lodge to
house both the dining area and space for the main meeting.
Together these facilities would provide enough space for their
first conference season. It would work. Their dream was fast
becoming reality.

Winter of 1945 was a time of hope. Not only had the
McNeills begun an exciting journey, but the century's second
great war appeared to near an end. Along with the rest of the

country, Evangeline and Archie looked forward to the end of the conflict. But they worried about the effect returning soldiers would have on the U.S. economy. Would the influx of unemployed men cause the value of the dollar to fall? Concerned, they saved every nickel in an effort to pay off the conference center property as soon as possible.

Forming a board of directors, they established the non-profit status of the ministry. While the McNeills owned the land and building privately, the corporation made plans to purchase the property as soon as the funds became available. Next they considered writing their purpose statement. With much prayer, they asked the Lord, "What is your plan for our ministry? What do you wish to accomplish here?" In time, they chose these words:

"Cannon Beach Christian Conference Center is interdenominational and works with the Church-at-Large. It presents the Word of God in its entirety and its simplicity. It challenges Christians to *consistent* Christian living, thus strengthening the spiritual life of the Church-at-Large. It stresses the Word of God, the walk with God, witnessing and missions."

As the McNeills continued their evangelism campaigns in local churches, they introduced the new ministry. They solicited both financial and physical help. A small lumber mill in central Oregon was the first to donate materials for structural repairs. Archie, Walter, and Haldane spent hours repairing the buildings.

The years of Coast Guard use had been hard on all of the structures. They had windows to replace, roofs that leaked and large holes in interior walls. The men began the backbreaking work of jacking up the log cabin in order to replace the lower logs, rotten from contact with the damp soil at the base of the building.

They added heating and new lighting. Though Archie had little experience with the practicalities of renovation,

Evangeline's brother, Walter always envisioned some clever and cost-saving solution to the latest problem. While the men pounded, the ladies painted. Together, the repair team moved toward the opening season.

Evangeline planned the summer schedule to begin on the 16th of July, 1945. By opening so late in the summer, they hoped to avoid the uncertain spring weather of the Oregon coast. She planned four, one-week conferences. The first and the third weeks would be especially for the women of the Christian Business and Professional Women's Clubs and Councils. Room and board for a one-week conference would total $16.50.

While advertising the conference center, Evangeline's years with the Duff Gospel Trio came in handy. She designed and printed modest brochures, which went with them wherever she and Archie traveled.

Desperate to keep cost of operating the ministry to an absolute minimum, Evangeline recruited volunteers to provide guest services. She found people to cook and serve meals. She found others to do dishes and clean rooms. She invited a friend to operate the reception desk. She found someone with experience to maintain the books and receive donations. She enlisted others to help with the grounds.

These volunteers were people she knew, people interested in the ministry, people willing to invest themselves in an opportunity to share the gospel with others. They were relatives, friends, former church members, or young people. Some met Evangeline as she traveled for the Christian Business and Professional Women's Clubs and Councils.

With the end of the war in sight, Archie resigned from the Serviceman's Center and the McNeills made their permanent home on the conference grounds.

At last ready, Archie and Evangeline received the very first registration by mail. Someone wanted to spend a week with them by the ocean!

When fall came, they considered their first summer a delightful success. All four week-long sessions had been full.

Archie and Evangeline worked hard to make their guests feel as though they were visiting a private home rather than a conference grounds. They hosted picnics at Ecola Park. Archie taught his guests to ride horses on the beach. Evangeline took others on scenic hikes. They welcomed conference visitors personally and often walked them to their car to say good-bye.

The short four-week season had been exhausting. Not only did Archie and Evangeline serve as host and hostess, but they also cleaned, cooked and shopped for groceries. At the same time, they paid bills, washed laundry, and cared for their own family. Whatever the volunteers left undone, the McNeills completed.

Though they were tired, they also experienced the exhilaration of success. After that first season, they felt absolutely certain about God's new direction for their lives. Guests left excited and grateful for the week at the beach. And, after the season closed, Evangeline and Archie were overwhelmed when two men approached them with a suggestion for expansion.

"This conference center is a wonderful gift of God. It must grow," they said. "You need to build a dining hall large enough to prepare and serve many more guests. If you can get the materials, we will help you build the building."

Though they found confirmation in the words, Archie and Evangeline already struggled to make monthly property payment of $200. How could they afford to build an additional building? One of the men, a builder, agreed to draw up the lumber order. Archie and Evangeline agreed to ask a supplier if he would sell the lumber wholesale.

Together, Archie and Evangeline went to visit Mr. Ben Ellis, a lumberman, in his Corvallis home. While they explained their mission, he listened attentively. After looking at their lumber order, the lumberman handed the sheet of paper to his wife. She read it slowly and returned the sheet without a word. The silence grew heavy. Finally, Mr. Ellis spoke, "My wife and I would like to donate the entire lumber order as a gift."

This was more than Archie and Evangeline had ever imagined and they thanked Mr. Ellis profusely. With much enthusiasm they returned to the coast. How faithfully God had met their needs!

Soon after, they experienced another proof of God's faithfulness. In January, Archie ordered a large collection of peeler logs from a local paper mill, having prayed that the sale of his Portland home would provide the funds to pay for them. Since the wood was cheap and sturdy, they planned to use the peeler logs as exterior lumber for the new dining hall. The mill would contact Archie when the half-logs became available.

About this time, the buyer of their Portland home began defaulting on his monthly payments. Archie and Evangeline didn't have extra money. They began to hope the mills wouldn't find the logs they needed. Then the call came. The logs were ready. They would need to pay for them at the time of delivery

Their hearts were heavy with worry until the next day in prayer; Evangeline had a verse of scripture come alive for her. "My God shall supply all your needs according to his riches in glory." With tears, she showed the verse to Archie.

The next day they went to Portland to see the buyer of their house.

The buyer greeted them with a pleasant welcome, saying, "Mr. McNeill, I want to consolidate my obligations. By tomorrow, I will pay the full amount due on the house." As they drove back to the coast, they realized—the amount due on the house contract exactly matched the amount needed to clear the bill on the half-logs!

As fall turned to winter, Archie continued to speak, traveling from church to church. Everywhere he shared his vision for the conference center. Whenever possible, Evangeline and Isabelle traveled with him.

They planned a work party for the spring of 1946. A fair-sized group of men joined Archie, Evangeline and the two men who spearheaded the dining hall idea. Evangeline cooked. Archie and the men built. When they were ready for the roof, they prayed together for clear weather—a bold request for March on the Oregon coast. The day dawned with summer-like sunshine. The men completed the roof.

The next summer, the conference center season opened with a brand new two-story dining hall. The upper floor housed two large dormitory areas. The main floor of the 40-by-80 building housed the kitchen and dining room and a small reception area. They named the building Ecola.

The "Work Week" crew for the spring of 1947 found themselves building a new chapel building, also of peeler logs. The number of guest weeks increased, as did attendance. The McNeills worked constantly to stay ahead of their growing ministry.

They established a mailing list of conference friends. They moved the small Coast Guard buildings to the back of the property and built another small guest building. To their delight, other church groups began to request the conference center as a location for private retreats. The McNeills accommodated these events during non-conference weeks. Any small increase in income helped to defray their overhead.

Archie and Evangeline began to hire help. They added a caretaker, and a summer cook. Gradually, a small staff of paid workers supported the volunteers. Still Archie and Evangeline worked tirelessly to keep the small operation going.

As they struggled to provide new space for the growth they experienced, the old buildings demanded care and attention, with needs such as new foundations, new floors, or new shakes.

They discovered, to their surprise, that the new living space over the dining room had one serious drawback. When people walked upstairs during dinner, the sand caked to their shoes came sifting down through the single layer floor onto the dining tables below. People came to the conference center to enjoy the beach—but not in their food! Another layer of flooring was immediately added above the dining room.

Though the conference center required enormous amounts of energy, Archie and Evangeline found their work very satisfying. This was their place, their calling. Archie, with his charming public manner, made the ideal conference director. Evangeline, with her ability to plan and oversee the conference details, served as his perfect complement.

Together they seemed ideally chosen for this exciting, though exhausting ministry. Everyone who knew them agreed. Surely God brought this pair together for this purpose. What great things they could accomplish!

Chapter Eleven

Alone

༒

*M*ISSIONARY. Evangeline printed neat capital letters in the space designated for occupation, quite pleased with her choice. It had taken a great deal of time for her to come to this decision. Though most would not find this question difficult, it was not a small thing to Evangeline. She smiled as she brushed away a tear.

In the eight months since Archie's death, she had wrestled with her new role. What was she? Conference Director? Evangelist? Pastor? Women's Club Organizer? Evangeline cared about words and she wanted to find the right term for her new role in life. Missionary seemed to say it all. No matter what position she filled, Evangeline knew that her life's purpose was to bring people to the Savior.

This tax form held great significance; it was the first she would file without Archie's help. Somehow, it signified both the end and the beginning. A dividing line in her life.

Missionary. Yes. That seemed to say it.

She wrote these words on April 15, 1953. She had put off filing her income taxes, and would have to hurry to finish the forms and get them in the mail. Many of the spaces on this year's form held new information. Evangeline had lived through a year of change.

The space where last year she had printed, "married," now held the word "widowed." Where last year she wrote Archie's name, this year she simply wrote, "deceased." Who would think so much pain could be found on an income tax form?

But more than labels had changed since last year. The woman returning to the Oregon coast in the spring of 1953 was different as well. Evangeline had grown stronger, more determined. She knew the leading of God in her life. He had, unmistakably, led her to this point. To this place. Under these conditions. She would not give up. She would not surrender. She had a strong Christian heritage. Her family stood ready to help at a moment's notice. With Haldane in Seattle and Walter in Dallas, Oregon she would get by.

She had planned the summer conference schedule while in Misouri. Helen's staff had helped Evangeline prepare and mail the advertisements and brochures. Now that she was back in Cannon Beach, Evangeline had only to carry out the season. With faith and determination, she went to work.

Not long into that first season without Archie, Evangeline made some striking discoveries. Archie had touched people everywhere, in all walks of life. He was alive in their memories. Since his death, Evangeline received more than 1,500 condolence messages. These people, who cared about Archie, now cared about the ministry of the conference center. It represented a way for people who loved Archie, to act out their love.

These people came from everywhere. They volunteered to put an addition on the chapel in his memory. They donated money to the ministry. They gave of their time and talents and resources. Whatever the conference center needed, they gave.

Certainly, Evangeline continued to grieve. Everything in Cannon Beach seemed to remind her that he was gone. Here was his favorite chair. There was someone riding on the beach—exactly the way he had ridden. She missed him terribly. Alive, Archie had helped her with every conference center decision. Now, she had to think through problems alone. She missed his practical approach to life.

But during this first season, Evangeline also discovered something even more remarkable. In the Bible, she found new significance in God's promise to be a "father to the fatherless, a defender of the widows" (Psalms 68:5). Evangeline took confidence waiting for the Lord's solutions to her problems, reasoning simply, *If God chose to put me in this place of leadership alone, then I can depend on Him to meet my every need.*

Reflecting this simple philosophy, Evangeline made every detail a matter of genuine, earnest prayer. Whether great or small, she prayed about everything. Then, as soon as she lifted her head from prayer, she began to look for His answer.

Evangeline believed she could depend on God for anything from parking places to lumber, from groceries to refrigerators. It wasn't as if Evangeline had any other source. God was her sole supply. And He would use whatever means He chose to provide for her. Evangeline found great joy in His answers.

With each answer, her confidence grew. She began to see that God often used people to meet her needs. All kinds of people. Many were Christians. Some were not. She began to have the courage to make her needs known to both Christians and non-Christians alike. Evangeline was rarely disappointed.

Volunteers built what came to be called the Administration building using lumber from the torn-down school. Evangeline placed her office on the main floor of the new structure. Every day, as she unlocked the door to her office, she was reminded of God's unfailing provision of materials and labor. That reminder gave her courage to keep going.

Though she wondered if this extraordinary support would ebb as the memory of Archie dimmed, Evangeline decided to enjoy it for as long as it might last.

Surprisingly, the support continued as conference center attendance increased. Every winter Evangeline returned to the Christian Women's Clubs headquarters in Missouri, where she planned the summer conference. Every spring she returned to the coast to supervise the summer conferences.

By the summer of 1956, two weeks of youth camps were added to the conference schedule, one for junior-high children, the other for high-school youth. More than three hundred teens attended each camp. In one case, two carloads of children were driven out from Colorado to attend.

Evangeline hired a local pastor to serve as director for these camps while her own staff planned the activities and provided for the camper's physical needs. Once again, many young people came to know Christ.

The success of the youth camps brought a new problem to Evangeline's attention. With the unpredictable weather on the Oregon coast, Evangeline struggled to keep 300 teenagers entertained. Because they could not always play outside, she decided that the conference center needed a large recreational-type building for youth activities. With that in mind, she set out to build a gymnasium.

Though she had volunteer help, she could not afford building supplies. Bankers, she discovered, would not consider loans to the conference center. On one such inquiry, the banker told her briskly, "We don't lend to 'fly by night' nonprofit organizations." Evangeline decided she would never ask for a loan again.

Several conference friends encouraged her to contact a Portland lumberman. Hesitant to ask a complete stranger for help, Evangeline bathed the suggestion in prayer. Finally, she called Mr. George Miller at his mill. When the call went through, he was not at the office. She called him at home. In a gruff tone he asked, "What do you want?"

Carefully, Evangeline explained the work of the conference center and her need to purchase a great deal of lumber to build a new gym. She closed with the request to purchase the lumber wholesale. Abruptly Mr. Miller asked, "Who are you? Are you Archie McNeill's wife?"

Mrs. McNeill responded positively.

He went on, "And are you Reverend Walter Duff's daughter?"

Again, Evangeline said that she was.

"Send me the lumber order by mail. It is yours."

With the gift of lumber, Evangeline asked for volunteers to build the gym. When the men arrived, they were delighted to discover that Evangeline could handle a hammer as well as anyone. She helped to nail the floorboards of the gym in place herself.

Evangeline had prayed and asked for help. And the help had come. On Sunday, July 22, 1956, she and conference center friends dedicated the new 100-by-56-foot building, which housed a 40-by-80-foot gym, a lounge and restrooms. The Lord had provided the gym; Evangeline rejoiced in that certainty.

Those who worked with Evangeline soon learned that there was no job she would not do. She painted. She cooked. She cleaned toilets. It never surprised the kitchen staff when Evangeline dropped by to peel potatoes with them. Then, with some bit of advice to the cook, she went off to her other responsibilities.

In spite of Archie's absence, Evangeline's work brought deep satisfaction. Her energy level seemed to multiply with every expansion of the facilities. She knew who she could count on for help and she depended heavily on them.

Her bookkeeper helped manage financial details. She had great trust in her handyman and a carpenter friend of the conference center. She found a designer who drew plans for the buildings she envisioned. These men answered her call again and again. Together, they made the conference center dream a growing reality.

While Evangeline supervised the growing conference center ministry, she did her best to raise Isabelle and Helen Jean. Though her mother helped, without Archie it was no easy task. Isabelle, now in her mid-teens, abhorred her given name. "The kids make such horrible nicknames out of it," she cried. "I want to choose a new name."

Evangeline understood the pain of awkward nicknames. She had lived through the same misery. The little family agreed to listen carefully for a new name for Isabelle.

Helen Jean, then in the second grade, came up with the solution. One day she arrived home from school, bounced into the kitchen and announced that she had found the perfect name for her big sister. "There is a new girl in my class," she confided, "and her name is Heather. Isn't that the most beautiful name? I think that we should change Isabelle's name to Heather."

Isabelle agreed that the name was perfect. But she wondered how to accomplish the change. Evangeline had the answer. The next time they enrolled Isabelle in a new school, they would register her as Heather. Since they changed schools twice each year, they would accomplish the task in no time. Isabelle Duff McNeill became Heather Duff McNeill.

In spite of the conference center's growth, the next year brought more sadness. In March of 1957, Evangeline's mother, Mathilda Hamilton Duff, passed away.

Evangeline suffered great personal loss with Mathilda's death. She had spent many of her last years with Evangeline and the girls. She helped Evangeline through losing Archie. Year after year, they had made the trip back and forth between Stonecroft in Missouri and the Oregon coast. Mathilda supervised the children while Evangeline traveled for Christian Women's Clubs and Councils.

Haldane, Evangeline's younger brother, recognized her sorrow and arranged to spend a few days with her after the funeral. Together they took long hikes on the beach, visiting, and remembering. Returning one day from the beach, they passed the ramshackle remains of the Cannon Beach Recreation Center. Haldane paused, looking at it as if he had never seen the building before.

"You know, Evangeline," he said, "You should buy this property for the conference center. What a beautiful location! Right on the oceanfront—just a block from the grounds. Perhaps a dining hall, the view is breathtaking!"

Though he said nothing more, Evangeline long believed such innocent comments—a passing suggestion, a phrase dropped inadvertently—often served as God's way of speaking to her. She brought the idea to the Lord in prayer. "Is this from you Lord? Please let me know."

Unable to free herself from the idea, she began to investigate the property. The owner happened to be spending the winter in Cannon Beach. She called him and made an appointment to see the building.

Mr. Mahon was very happy to show her the property. As they passed through the building, he told Evangeline how this could be altered or that could be fixed.

As he prattled on, Evangeline wondered, *How does one wreck a building?*

Unfortunately, Mr. Mahon did not have all the building keys with him. So they agreed to meet again the next day to view the rest of the property. As they parted, Mr. Mahon told Evangeline, "For only $20,000, you can have the four lots, the swimming pool and the buildings."

Evangeline spent a troubled night. To her, the pool presented nothing more than a safety hazard. The building needed to be demolished. And, of course, there was the small issue of money. She didn't have $20,000. For that matter, she didn't have $200. "Lord," she prayed, "is this your arrangement or mine?"

Then the thought came to her. "Offer him $15,000 cash. If he agrees to the twenty-five percent reduction in price, you will know the property is from me." Settled in her course, she slept peacefully through the rest of the night.

The next day, she and Mr. Mahon met at the appointed hour. As he was unlocking the door, she said, "Mr. Mahon, before we look further, I just want you to know what happened last night. I prayed about this and I am going to offer you $15,000 cash. If you accept, then I know God wants us to have the property. If you don't take the offer, there will be no hard feelings. I will know it is not for us."

With that he snapped the lock closed. Evangeline, worried that she had offended him, said quietly, "I'll walk myself home."

"No, no, get into the car," he replied.

He did not speak until they were back to the conference center. "Mrs. McNeill, what did you say to me?"

She repeated the offer.

"Well, I don't own the property myself. My wife and mother-in-law also have an interest. I will talk with them." With that, he drove away.

Evangeline believed that she would never hear from him again. An hour later, she answered a knock at the front door. Surprised to see Mr. Mahon so soon, she invited him in. Her surprise turned to amazement when he told her that the family had agreed to her offer. "I'm on my way to Portland right now to see our attorney," he told her.

As she closed the door behind him, Evangeline stood in a state of shock. "Father, what do we do now?" The conference center had not a penny for the purchase of additional land. At least now, she had confirmation of the Lord's leading. The Lord would just have to provide the funds as well.

When Archie died in 1952, some friends told Evangeline they would be glad to loan her money if she ever had the need. In the past, she had borrowed small amounts in order to start the summer season. She wondered if perhaps these same friends would consider another loan for the purchase of property. The next morning she drove to visit them in Corvallis, Oregon.

"Mrs. McNeill, you know I would be glad to loan you the money. But I don't have any to loan at this minute. A man owes me $5,000. But, he has even defaulted on the interest payments. There is little hope in that."

Disappointed, Evangeline stood to leave.

"Let's pray before you go," her friend said. "You know, Evangeline, I think I'll go speak to the man who owes me money."

Evangeline returned to Cannon Beach via Portland where she stopped to visit another friend who might be able to help. Unfortunately, he was away on vacation. Resigned that she could do nothing more, Evangeline headed for the coast.

When she arrived, her Corvallis friend called her. "You will never believe what happened," he said. "I went to see the man who owes me money, and without an explanation, he gave me a check for the entire $5,000. It must be the answer to our prayer! The check is in the mail. It should be in Cannon Beach by tomorrow."

Though grateful, Evangeline realized that $5,000, no matter how miraculous, was not $15,000. Where would she find the additional $10,000? She spent the rest of the evening thanking and praising the Lord for His miracle. At the same time she asked. "What next?"

Early the next morning, Mr. Mahon returned to visit Evangeline. She could see that he was agitated. Evangeline waited for him to explain.

"Mrs. McNeill," he blurted, "my attorney tells me I cannot sell that property for cash. All I can take is $5,000 down, and the remainder must be paid at $3,000 per year."

Evangeline could hardly maintain enough decorum to see him to the door. Then Evangeline burst into her own private praise party. Once again God had managed the impossible. He had arranged a property sale for 75 percent of the asking price and then, to her surprise, provided the finances to close the deal. God managed all of this without Evangeline having a single penny in the bank.

Did God want her to have the recreation center property? Evangeline knew the answer. Yes. Absolutely.

At the same time, Evangeline had another dream simmering away in her mind. Conference attendance continued to climb. She had opened every season with the Christian Businessmen's Conference, followed by a week for a Village Missions Retreat. After this, she held one of her youth weeks. The other youth week was tucked away at the end of the summer, just before Labor Day weekend.

The "new" chapel and dining hall, built just 10 years before, enabled the conference center to host many more guests for chapel services and meals than it could accommodate in guest housing. She struggled to house the people who wanted to stay on the conference grounds. She believed that the conference center needed more guest rooms.

So, she approached her friend and designer Gordon Nickell. Together, they made plans to build an eight-unit building near the new gymnasium. Their goal was to construct additional family housing, making it as deluxe as possible on a very limited budget. The rooms would be spacious—eighteen feet from partition to partition. And, most exciting of all, each room would contain a bathroom with a shower! Never before had the conference center considered including such luxury.

Once again, the purchase of materials would be the most difficult part of adding another building. The conference center did not charge its summer guests enough to cover its operations, let alone allow Evangeline to save toward additional building capital. Evangeline decided to contact her friend and lumber dealer, Mr. Miller. Once again, he graciously provided the needed lumber. By the summer of 1957, they opened eight new units near the creek, calling the new building "The Anchorage."

The new units were a success from the moment they were opened. Once again, demand outstripped supply. With careful thought, they considered removing an old warehouse, which was between the new unit and the main grounds. Without the warehouse, the new Anchorage could be continued, giving them six additional units. Again Gordon Nickell drew plans.

Later that summer, Haldane delivered bad news. He had read of Mr. George Miller's death in the Portland paper. The loss of her gruff, but faithful lumber friend saddened Evangeline. She wrote a long letter of sympathy to Mrs. Miller. "We, at the conference center, have been so very grateful for all his gifts of lumber. I have often heard much about his endeavors for the Lord. He was certainly a prince among men."

At Christmas that year, Mrs. McNeill received a Christmas card signed, "Your dead friend, George Miller."

In his note, George explained the coincidence—that a man with the same name had died. "Your letter was certainly a surprise to my wife, but she has recovered nicely. Not many men have the good fortune of reading their own letters of condolence. But I assure you; I appreciated the many fine things you said about me. And, Mrs. McNeill, if you have any further need of lumber, you have only to let me know."

In the summer of 1959, the conference center opened six additional units in the Anchorage building. Needless to say, they were built with lumber donated by Mr. Miller, who was very much alive.

Evangeline came to the end of that summer season with a great sense of peace. Yes, the decade had been a difficult one. She had experienced great loss. But, she had also known the pleasure and satisfaction of being in the very center of God's will. She had witnessed His miraculous provision. She knew His guidance. An exciting new decade stretched out before her. She knew that God would continue to lead and provide.

Evangeline sensed a season of growth waiting for her and for the work. Yes, she very much looked forward to the new year.

CHAPTER TWELVE

A Change for Nick

*T*hough he felt great fear, Nick entered the Umatilla County Courthouse with a sense of dread. It was clear, even to his 12-year-old mind that he was in big trouble. Charged with vandalism and burglary, Nick recognized the seriousness of this court hearing. Still, when he saw his father in the courtroom, he hoped that something good might come of it all.

Nick had only seen his father in a suit once before—at the funeral. Everyone wore a suit to a funeral. But here was Nick's father, dressed in his brown suit. Nick shuddered with a mixture of fear and anticipation.

He hoped that his father's presence marked the beginning of something new in their family—a new commitment—a new presence. Maybe the judge would slap Nick's hands and turn him over to the custody of his father. Maybe now, in spite of so much pain, Dad would really try to build a family.

After the judge pronounced the sentence Nick turned to his father. Hoping for something, some consolation, some encouragement, Nick looked deep into his father's eyes. The forgiveness he longed for was missing.

Instead he saw his father's face tense with anger. "You are not my son," he said. "You never were my son. You're nothing. If you ever get out of there, don't you ever come back. You'll never live in my house again."

Though deeply disappointed, the outburst did not surprise Nick. This was the father he knew best. He heard truth in his father's words. There was no hope for their relationship. No hope for Nick. He had been cast adrift and now he was completely alone.

Alone, he watched the green door of his steel cage slam shut. As the footsteps of the guard softened into the background, Nick found himself facing a single steel bed, a steel sink, and toilet—and a cascade of memories. At least he had plenty of time to think.

His mind drifted back over the years, and he wondered why he found this solitude so painful. For as long as he could remember, Nick and his brothers and sisters had been on their own. How many times had his mother left home with a new man? How many times had alcohol taken his father away? How many nights, holidays, and weekends had the children been left without food? Without clothing. Without love.

Looking out of the small window in his cell, he pondered the twinkling lights which marked the homes in the valley below. As the twilight deepened, the lights grew brighter. Each light a home, he thought, a face, a family.

Then as the stars began to appear in the darkness, Nick was drawn to the enormity of the universe. If there was a God, His creation was immense, diverse.

Again a memory returned to him. On the day of his brother's funeral, Nick had seethed with anger toward God. How could a good God allow such a tragic death? Nick had wondered how he would ever live without Tom.

Tom had been the only goodness in their family. Before he died, Tom told Nick he had become a Christian. Nick didn't understand what Tom meant, but he clearly recognized the difference it made in Tom's life. Some God, Nick had concluded. He lets His own people die.

Then Nick remembered having a strange, almost comforting experience at the funeral. Sitting in the service, Nick had heard a voice.

"It's all right Nick. It's OK. He's with me."

The voice seemed so real that Nick remembered looking around to find the one who had spoken.

Now, in his jail cell, as the twilight deepened into blackness, Nick wondered again about the voice. Had he really heard God?

As a child, Nick occasionally attended Sunday school. His teacher had taught him about God and sin. He remembered that God forgave sin. Certainly, he reasoned, the long list of charges the police officer had read in court constituted sin.

As the nighttime hours passed, the broken teenager told God everything he had done. Then as dawn began to break, Nick said, "God, if you could forgive me, I need it. And if you could do anything with this life, I give it to you. I'll do anything you ask. And God, if you could love me, I really need that, too."

When the sun came up, Nick found himself sitting in the very lap of God, experiencing the wonderful blanket-like hug that only God can give a hungry soul.

When Nick left the courthouse the next day bound for the MacLaren Reform School, he was a changed boy. Though he was handcuffed, his heart was finally free.

Reform school in the early 1960s was a prison-like experience, including total control and regular humiliation by the staff. One day, the warden called Nick to his office, and offered him the opportunity to be released to a foster home.

With more than one hundred boys waiting for placement, Nick knew his name had been on the bottom of the list. However, for some unexplainable reason, Nick's name had suddenly been moved to the top of the list. Though he had no understanding of what a foster home might entail, Nick could hardly wait to get out of reform school. Without hesitation, he agreed.

Lee Huffsmith, who ran a Portland foster home with Youth for Christ, became Nick's first foster mother. In her home, Nick learned how real Christianity worked in the family environment. Through Lee, Nick met Evangeline McNeill.

One spring day, Lee and Nick headed for the Oregon coast in a new '64 Chevy station wagon. As they turned onto the conference grounds, its pristine beauty struck Nick. He had never experienced beauty for beauty's sake. All around the conference grounds, flowers and gardens and grass flourished, just for the beauty of it all.

Then from across the grounds, he saw Evangeline McNeill, her red hair carefully coiled up on top of her head. She moved quickly, with purpose. In a neatly pressed blouse and skirt, she smiled and waved. She seemed genuine enough. Though Nick and Lee were unexpected guests, Evangeline McNeill greeted them with graciousness and genuine warmth.

At this point, 13-year-old Nick was tentative. Institutional living had driven out any feeling of self-worth. Yet Mrs. McNeill seemed genuinely glad to meet him, so full of effervescence. His gratitude for her kindness soon grew into deep respect and love.

The two women talked about summer employment for the four foster boys from the Huffsmith home. Lee wondered if they could serve as kitchen help. In spite of their delinquent background, Evangeline seemed delighted to have the boys join her staff.

One month later, all four boys found themselves working long days as part of the conference dishwasher crew. In a hot kitchen with less than optimal equipment the boys lived wet, greasy lives. Their wrinkled fingers soon resembled prunes.

Because of their background, Evangeline kept a special eye on the boys, checking frequently to see that their needs were met. After a short time, she began to ask Nick to accompany her on her evening rounds. In the dark, as Evangeline locked the buildings, they shared bits and pieces of their past. Soon, Evangeline knew all about his lonely childhood, and the activity that brought Nick to the Huffsmith home.

Evangeline amazed Nick. She seemed to oversee every detail of conference life. Her hands were part of every task. No matter how small or dirty, Nick found Evangeline involved in every job. Soon she asked the boys to help in other areas of ministry.

On one particular evening Evangeline arrived in the kitchen in her evening formal. She was scheduled to play a concert harp solo for the evening service. Nick expected her to come in and check on their progress with the evening cleanup. Instead, Evangeline opened the refrigerator and removed an entire bag of clean carrots. With knife in hand, chopping furiously, she said, "Dear, can you give me a hand with these carrots?"

Together they chopped. Then, as suddenly as she arrived, she dried her hands and left for the chapel. Nick watched her hurry across the grounds to perform for the chapel guests. From her meticulous appearance, the guests would have no idea she came from working in the kitchen.

Within minutes, Evangeline was back, furiously chopping carrots. Nick soon discovered that Evangeline's willingness to help in the kitchen extended to every job on the grounds. Whatever she asked the boys to do, she worked alongside of them.

As the summer progressed, the special friendship between Evangeline and Nick grew. Nick accompanied her on her weekly trips to Portland. Though the conference center had grown considerably, Evangeline still bought all the groceries herself. Every week she took the little green truck, outfitted with stock racks, to Portland. On these trips they often picked up other supplies—plywood, Formica, moldings, or any other building supply the operation needed. The trips exhausted young Nick.

But he looked forward to the time alone with Evangeline. Week after week, as they headed up the highway, they would sing some and talk a great deal. Nick would ask questions about the Lord, about Christianity and his new faith, and especially about things he had observed at the center. Lovingly and patiently, Evangeline began to build an understanding of the depth and scope of Nick's new faith in Christ.

On one particular summer day as they began their weekly trip Evangeline announced that she needed 13 watermelons. Without hesitation she simply stopped and prayed aloud for her watermelons. Nick groaned.

Oh come on, NOBODY prays for watermelons.

The day progressed as usual. They purchased Formica, curtain hardware, and bathroom fixtures. Then they went to pick up the week's groceries. With their purchases carefully stuffed into the truck, they climbed into the truck cab. Having spent all their money, they had purchased no watermelons. Nick didn't mention Evangeline's unanswered prayer, but he felt sure they would head home without them.

Just then Jimmy, the market owner, came toward the truck. "Mrs. McNeill," he said, "would you have any use for watermelon? I have 13 out back that you can have if you can use 'em."

Nick went home that day with a new understanding of everyday faith.

He loved to attend the evening services and often hurried through the dishes to arrive in the chapel just as the speaker took the podium. Like a sponge, Nick soaked up the rich teaching of great Bible teachers from all over the country. But his favorite event occurred after the service, when the regular guests left.

Frequently, Evangeline invited the speaker to her home for tea. Always she included Nick. Though he never understood why she invited a 13-year-old to these adult gatherings, he relished every opportunity to listen to the personal stories of the wonderful speakers who came to the conference.

One night, the speaker, Dr. John Moore, was full of questions for Nick. "Of all the things you could get in your life, what would you want most?"

Nick answered, "I really don't have a decent Bible, and I'm a new Christian. I'd love to own a Scofield Bible."

Not long after, Dr. Moore sent his own Scofield Study Bible to Nick. The inside cover was inscribed "To John M. Moore, Glasgow, Scotland." The book was filled with his personal sermon and study notes. Nick devoured the margin notes and carefully followed the studies. That summer Nick came to feel deep respect and admiration for those in ministry.

Though Nick moved from foster home to foster home, every summer he returned to Cannon Beach. Quitting his part-time winter job, he would head for a much less profitable job at the coast. As the summers progressed, Nick found himself leading the singing and playing trumpet solos for the conference guests. His special relationship with Evangeline continued to grow.

He developed friendships that included other members of the staff. David Duff, a nephew of Evangeline and son of Village Missions director Walter Duff, became an especially close friend.

Each fall he returned to school, until at age 15, the state of Oregon discontinued his supervision and financial support. Determined to finish school, he returned to the Huffsmith home and rented a room. By pumping gas, and repairing and delivering copy machines, Nick made enough to survive. As graduation grew near, he faced the reality that college, for him, was out of the question. His only reasonable choice appeared to be a military career. Nick began testing for enrollment in flight school.

Evangeline, however, had other plans. She told him with certainty that he should be preparing himself for full-time ministry. As she spoke, Nick recognized the truth of her words. But to him the situation seemed hopeless. With no money, and no place to stay, Bible school seemed an unattainable goal.

After his high school graduation, Nick returned again to the conference center. Late that summer, he helped in the evening chapel service as usual. After he led the worship and the special music had begun, Evangeline took him aside and asked him to go over to the kitchen and check on dessert preparation.

Her request was so unusual that Nick hesitated slightly. After he returned from the kitchen, he took the evening offering. Later, after three different men asked to meet Nick, he discovered what Evangeline had been up to.

While Nick was in the kitchen, she spoke to the congregation. "I believe God wants that young man in ministry. He needs to attend Bible school this fall, and I believe that some family here could help by providing a place for him to stay."

Less than two weeks later, Nick, a tall robust man with sensitive deep brown eyes, entered Bible school in Eugene, Oregon. Four years later, Nick and his bride assumed their first pastoral position with Village Missions in Hawk Springs, Wyoming.

CHAPTER THIRTEEN

Bits and Pieces

A ringing telephone interrupted Wanda's thoughts. "Ugh," she said, backing out on her hands and knees, "why does that thing only ring when I am in the middle of something?" Ignoring the pain in her joints, she stood up, and removed her rubber gloves. The floor was half washed. Oh well. She dashed for the phone.

"Hello Wanda, honey. This is Evangeline."

Her irritation turned to delight. As Village Missionaries working in Bridge, Oregon, Neil and Wanda Fisher had known Evangeline a long time. Wanda considered Evangeline a good friend.

Evangeline explained that she was helping to start a Christian Woman's Club in Myrtle Point, Oregon. Wanda smiled. She had been involved in these kinds of plans before. Normally, a luncheon featured a guest speaker and some draw—a demonstration, or a style show.

"I'm planning the luncheon," Evangeline said. "And you know Wanda, when I was at your house the last time, you made the most delicious cinnamon twists. I wonder, could I ask you to make enough for 100 women? They would really dress up the plates."

Wanda gladly agreed to make the rolls. Active in Christian Women's Clubs herself, she believed in the ministry as a way to win women to Christ. Baking the twists would be no problem.

"And honey, do you think you could have some of the ladies from you church volunteer to help set up and clean up? Then, we'll need some ladies to host the tables and others to serve the meals."

Wanda chuckled to herself. Baking rolls was nothing compared to finding volunteers. "Sure, Mrs. McNeill. How many women do you need?"

After the phone call, Wanda did not see or hear from Evangeline again. On the day of the luncheon, at the appointed hour, Wanda met the other volunteers at the rented hall. Wanda was surprised to find that no one had yet begun to cook the food.

Just then, Mrs. McNeill drove up in her big green Oldsmobile. Jumping out of the driver's seat, she greeted the ladies and proceeded to open the trunk. There, to Wanda's amazement, was enough food to feed 100 ladies. With remarkable efficiency, Evangeline instructed the ladies in setting up tables and decorating the hall.

While the ladies decorated the dining room, Evangeline went to the kitchen and prepared the food for the luncheon. Though Wanda had no idea who would be doing what, she certainly hadn't expected Evangeline to cook for that many people. Before long, delicious smells came wafting from the kitchen.

With both the dining room and the food ready, Evangeline called the volunteer servers into the kitchen and gave them last minute instructions. Then she disappeared into the restroom.

Moments later, Wanda happened to glance up as Evangeline emerged beautifully dressed and made-up, wearing a lovely luncheon hat. Then, she went to the front door and began to graciously greet her guests.

The program went completely as planned. The guests enjoyed themselves and the delicious food. At last, the hostess introduced the speaker. Who should get up to speak but Mrs. McNeill of Cannon Beach Christian Conference Center?

Wanda savored her secret. Wouldn't these ladies be surprised to know that the guest speaker was also the cook? Nothing about Mrs. McNeill's gracious composure gave any hint of the things she had done that morning. With a gentle opportunity to accept Jesus as Savior, the luncheon was closed. Unhurried, Mrs. McNeill chatted with the women as they exited the hall.

Just as Wanda and her crew finished clearing the tables, Mrs. McNeill joined them in the kitchen. Once again, she had changed clothes, leaving her luncheon hat behind. Before long, Evangeline was up to her elbows in dirty dishes.

Though the volunteers were tired, Wanda noticed that not one of them left the rented hall before Mrs. McNeill. They helped her load leftovers into her trunk, and warmly thanked her for all she had done.

As Wanda drove home, she pondered the afternoon's events. She had never seen anyone work harder, never seen a more gracious or humble effort to win women to Christ. Cook. Supervisor. Advertiser. Clean up. Guest speaker. Evangeline McNeill had done all these things without notice. Without fanfare.

After a long and exhausting day, Evangeline crawled into bed and fallen into a deep sleep. When she woke, she did not know how long the phone had been ringing. Her mind refused to respond. Her heavy limbs felt sluggish. At last she answered.

The voice on the other end rang with alarm. "My friend has run away. I tried to talk to him but he wouldn't listen." The male voice continued, "Please. Can you help me? He swallowed a full bottle of sleeping pills before he left. I think he's headed for the beach. I would go after him, but he needs someone who can do more. Someone who can get through to him. I called his parents and they said to call you. What can you do?" The voice rose in panic.

Wide-awake now, Evangeline answered. "We will pray and we will look," she said in a calm, reassuring voice. Giving whatever additional assurances she could think of, she hung up and crawled out of bed. Though she answered this kind of call all the time, she wondered what she should do for this boy. How could she help when his friend could not?

The people of Cannon Beach believed that Evangeline McNeill would help in any emergency—at any time of the day or night. Though she frequently responded to their calls, Evangeline knew where to find real help. As she dressed, she began to pray.

Once again the phone rang and Evangeline found herself listening to the missing boy's desperate mother. "We are on our way," she assured Evangeline. "But it will take us nearly three hours. Please," she begged, "do what you can."

Evangeline called her secretary. Though it was three hours after midnight, Lucille appeared at her door a few minutes later dressed and ready to help. Together they prayed as they walked to the car. Where would they look?

Driving along the beach was treacherous, even in the daylight. The two women agreed to start by checking downtown. As they turned onto Main Street, Evangeline's headlights caught a lone figure walking quickly along the sidewalk.

Mrs. McNeill slowed the car and rolled down her window. The figure slowed as well. She asked the young man's name. Without hesitation he gave it. They'd found him—dazed but coherent. Evangeline explained who she was and asked him to get into the car. Remarkably, the boy complied.

Understanding the importance of getting the boy to the hospital, Evangeline turned the car toward Seaside. As they passed the conference grounds, the boy became agitated. "Are you taking me to the hospital? I thought you said you were taking me to your place. I'm getting out right now."

Evangeline swung the car around saying, "We're going to my house. How about something hot to eat?"

Finding the house warm and cozy, the boy began to relax. Lucille fixed him some hot chocolate, while Evangeline called his parents. They had not yet left home.

As Evangeline was instructed, she called the doctor on duty at the Seaside Hospital. "You must not let him go to sleep under any circumstances," he urged her. "Call the police and have him brought right in."

After losing precious minutes contacting the police, she found them unwilling to help. "It is a matter for an ambulance," they told her. Desperate, Evangeline called for an ambulance. The boy had already fallen asleep.

The ambulance in Cannon Beach had gone on another call.

They could not get him into the car by themselves. She and Lucille prayed. The phone rang and Evangeline answered to find the ambulance leader on the end of the line. "We just finished our last call and heard you needed some help. What can we do?"

Evangeline explained the situation and within minutes the crew loaded the unconscious boy into the ambulance. She and Lucille followed him to the Seaside emergency room where the boy's stomach was pumped.

He survived the ordeal!

As an exhausted Evangeline drove her secretary back to the conference center, Lucille said sleepily, "You know Evangeline, you need to do something about being available to everyone in town whenever anyone needs you. You can't be out every night looking for runaways. You need your rest."

"Lucille," Evangeline answered calmly. "Where would that young man be if we hadn't been there tonight? I know you care. I appreciate that. And you're right. Maybe I can't keep up this schedule forever. But for now, I can. And, for as long as God asks me, I will be available."

The bedroom door opened quietly, letting in a soft glow as a small figure walked into the room. In an effort to wake up, Marty rolled over and stretched. After traveling all day, she was so tired. What could Evangeline possibly want now?

"You know, Marty, I love you so much," Evangeline whispered, kneeling beside the bed. She reached out and gently stroked Marty's hair. Moments later, she stood up and left the room, closing the door behind her.

Marty's eyes filled with tears. No matter how long she lived, she would never understand Evangeline's love. No one had ever loved Marty in this way. It felt so good, knowing that no matter what she looked like, what mischief she was in, Evangeline loved her.

Marty let her weary mind drift back over the years to her first visit to the conference center. She had just made a personal commitment to Christ. Since her own family rarely attended church, she had little opportunity to grow in her newfound faith. Marty's best friend had invited her to join her family for part of a week at the Cannon Beach Conference Center.

Marty remembered that week as one of the most wonderful weeks of her life. The speaker spent the entire time talking about Jesus. It had been so special that Marty determined she would return again the next year. And she had returned—every single year until she was old enough to join the summer staff.

During those years Heather McNeill befriended Marty and helped her get a summer job cleaning rooms at a motel near the conference center. But after she started work, Marty discovered that the motel owner was unwilling to let Marty attend church on Sunday. Marty was bitterly disappointed. When Heather told her mother, Evangeline responded by offering Marty a job waiting tables at the conference center. She accepted with delight.

Heather and Marty enjoyed a wild summer together. The 10 or 12 girls who lived above the administration office spent the summer dreaming about the boys on staff. They whispered and giggled, sang together and shared clothes. Marty realized that the young people who worked at the conference center were by no means perfect. Some were quite mature in their Christian faith. Others, like herself, were not.

A very attractive young woman, Marty had done some modeling in southern Oregon before coming to the conference center. In the last style show, her hairdresser had put a red streak in her hair. The other kids on staff saw it as a sign of Marty's worldliness. While they openly made unkind comments about her, Mrs. McNeill never had. Mrs. McNeill always made her feel like she was loved. Like she belonged.

During that first summer Marty worked very hard. And, as part of the summer activity, the "wait staff" was invited to join in the teaching sessions for the youth camp that occupied the last week of the summer. The speaker encouraged the youth to fully dedicate their lives to Jesus Christ. On the last night, he gave his audience an opportunity to come forward in dedication.

Marty wanted to respond. But she had endured so much teasing, she was reluctant to give the staff more ammunition. Then she felt a tap on the shoulder. She turned to find a boy smiling at her. "Why don't you go forward?" he said.

It was all the encouragement she needed.

She went home a changed young woman. She had never before wanted to give every part of herself to Jesus. After that week, Marty wanted to make a difference in her school. She would witness. She would let her friends know that she was a Christian.

Year after year, Marty returned to Cannon Beach, growing deep in her relationship to the Lord.

When Marty announced that she had entered her first beauty pageant, Mrs. McNeill was supportive despite her misgivings. Marty smiled to herself when she remembered Heather telling her what her mother said.

"How could anyone parade around in a bathing suit in front of an audience?"

Evangeline McNeill softened only when she realized how many new opportunities Marty would have to share her faith.

Alone in the dark, as Marty sorted through her memories, her smile turned into a quiet giggle. Yes, Mrs. McNeill had certainly figured out how to help Marty share her faith. After she became Miss Oregon 1962, Evangeline asked Marty to join her, driving around Oregon in Mrs. McNeill's big old Oldsmobile.

Some life of glamour. Every night a different town—a different church—a different home. Marty rolled over and groaned—a different bed.

Evangeline had planned their itinerary weeks before they left Cannon Beach. Though Marty knew she was nothing more than bait, that Evangeline was one of the world's greatest fishermen, Marty didn't mind. After four long weeks, she had lost track of the others who had joined them. An opera singer. A famous pianist.

At first, Marty begged Evangeline, "Don't make me put on my formal!" She hated the miserable confinement of the big, hooped evening dress.

"But dear," Evangeline countered, "many of these people have never seen anyone look as beautiful as you do—all dressed up in your formal. Do it for them."

Marty did it. Night after night she put on her beautiful dress and gave her testimony. Every night Evangeline followed with a little salvation message of her own.

The long road trip left Marty dead tired. Soon it would be over. She looked forward to spending two nights in the same bed. *Well,* she thought as she closed her eyes again, *it has certainly been an experience.* Marty had learned how to share her faith. She had grown more comfortable in front of an audience. And most importantly, some of Evangeline's zeal had rubbed off on Marty.

Marty smiled and whispered into the darkness. "I love you too, Evangeline."

CHAPTER FOURTEEN

Expansion

*s the decade of the sixties dawned, Evangeline saw so much potential in the conference center ministry. So many opportunities. In order to make those dreams come true, she would have to find a way to expand the facilities.

The original conference buildings, quickly aging, required constant upkeep. Less comfortable than the new Anchorage units, families rarely chose to stay in them. Evangeline realized that she needed to build new lodgings.

Early in the new decade, Evangeline arranged to have some of the dangerous outbuildings on the Rec Center property removed. Because a serious winter storm had destroyed most of the seawall that protected the village of Cannon Beach, the city required each ocean front property owner to pay for a new seawall. Though the expense was a hardship for the conference center, once again God provided the funds. Soon a new wall, built of log pilings, replaced the damaged seawall.

Because he lived so close, Walter became a valuable source of support and comfort for Evangeline. Many times, when a plane was delayed or a speaker became suddenly ill, Walter's phone would ring.

After Evangeline explained the dilemma, Walter lost no time in driving to the coast where he filled in for the missing speaker. More than this, Walter freely offered advice, found volunteers, or handled any unexpected emergency.

The strong ties in the Duff family enabled Evangeline to be a giver as well. Her brother, Haldane, had established a thriving conference ministry of his own in the Seattle area known as Park of the Pines. Haldane's ministry benefited by using many of the musicians and speakers his sister discovered. Whatever resources they had, they shared.

Nearly all of Evangeline's nieces and nephews spent summers working at the conference center. There, they gained friends, and took on new responsibilities. They learned new skills, and learned to think of Evangeline as a mother away from home. For most of the nieces and nephews, the conference center gave them their first opportunity to try their hand at working adult relationships. For some, it served as their first exposure to shoe-leather Christianity—outside the narrow circle of their immediate family.

Over the years Evangeline became friends with Edna Frisbee, the elderly widow of the man who originally owned the conference center property. Though Edna was the same age as Evangeline's mother, they enjoyed one another's company. As Mrs. Frisbee grew older, Evangeline would take her an occasional meal, or volunteer to drive her to a doctor's appointment. Evangeline worried about Edna's health—both because they were friends, and because Edna Frisbee still owned land adjacent to the conference center.

Often Evangeline spoke to Edna about the possibility of buying the remaining parcel. But Edna would never consider such a sale. "Oh, Evangeline, there will be plenty of time to worry about that," she would say.

Evangeline knew better. If Edna died without selling, it was possible that her heirs would not want to sell to the conference center.

When Mrs. Frisbee suddenly passed away, Evangeline was both surprised and saddened. She would miss the company of her friend, and the hours they spent together. When Mrs. Frisbee's attorney contacted Evangeline, she was even more surprised.

Though Edna Frisbee left a large portion of her estate to the Christian Science Church, she had named Mrs. Evangeline McNeill, "her devoted friend," as heir to the land adjacent to the conference center. In all their conversations Edna had never hinted that she would not sell because she always intended to leave it to Evangeline.

This new gift along with an unused strip of conference land formed a large parcel where Evangeline could now build additional guest facilities. It seemed that God had once again provided for the conference in a most miraculous way.

Rejoicing in the provision, she asked Gordon Nickell to design plans for a building that would fit the unusual angles of the property. He presented her with drawings for a new building in a large flying wedge shape—one that could be completed in three sections.

The first portion would face the inner garden area, with eight rooms on each floor. Each room, accessed by a rear hallway, had its own lanai with sliding patio doors. Private bathrooms and a garden view made these rooms the most luxurious the conference center had ever offered.

As usual, Mrs. McNeill began the building project without a single penny set aside. The money, materials, and labor would come in, she believed, as they were needed. They always had. They would again.

In January of 1963, while one volunteer crew repaired damage to the Anchorage roof, another poured the footings for the new lodge.

Like all those before it, the new building was built entirely by volunteer labor. When materials or workers were available, the project moved steadily forward. But whenever they ran short of supplies or men, the entire undertaking came to a halt. At times the lack of progress discouraged Evangeline.

However, each time things slowed down, Evangeline prayed. God always answered. To everyone's surprise, conference center guests used the first wing in the summer of 1963. Grateful for its completion, Evangeline wrote in her conference newsletter dated October 1963:

"Did you know the lumber for the new building was a gift? The architectural plans…a gift? The beautiful patio doors on the lower level…a gift? The plumbing need was met by interested friends who gave gifts of $100. The cement pouring was a gift. The electrical installation…a gift. The lighting fixtures…a gift, and Mr. Roland Casey, the contractor in charge, gave hours and hours of time and effort in dedication to the task, assisted by other gifted men."

She named the beautiful new motel-style building, provided entirely by the loving gifts and donated hours of many conference center friends, The Haven.

Pausing for only a moment to enjoy the success of the building project, Evangeline began planning to the next portion of the three-stage project. After securing the lumber, she stored it at the end of the property near the creek. Then in the spring of 1964, God Himself took a more active role in her building plans.

On the Friday of Holy Week, March 27, 1964, Evangeline made plans to celebrate the birthday of her good friend and staff member Winnie Argenbright. After sending Winnie into Seaside to an evening church service, Evangeline decorated her home for a surprise party. Winnie returned to a house full of well-wishers. They enjoyed a delicious cake, and there was much laughter. By eleven o'clock, everyone had gone. Evangeline retired.

Sometime later, Evangeline woke to pounding on her door. Reluctant to get up again, Evangeline wondered who had arrived so late? When at last she opened the door, she discovered Polly, a staff member. "Quickly, Mrs. McNeill, there is a tidal wave. There was an earthquake in Alaska, and we're just getting the water now. Hurry. The water is coming up."

Evangeline woke Winnie, and dressed in their night-clothes, the three women scurried up the ladder leaning against her carport. Safely perched on the roof, they watched with wonder as the water steadily rose. On a beautifully clear night, the full moon gave the eerie sensation of daylight.

A duplex floated up the creek and settled in the field across from the conference grounds. It was followed by the Ecola Creek Bridge.

The bridge did not fare nearly so well as the house. Broken into pieces, large logs floated by as they watched. The water continued to rise, and soon they realized that they would be stranded unless they escaped via the south end of town. Carefully the women climbed off the roof and headed by rowboat for higher ground. Evangeline spent a restless night at a friend's home.

When dawn broke, anxious to go back and account for the damage, Evangeline, Winnie and Polly returned to the grounds.

To their surprise, the water had caused very little damage to the buildings themselves. They would have to pull up and clean the carpets on the first floor of the new building. It seemed as if something had prevented the water from reaching the conference grounds. The women searched for an explanation. Remarkably they discovered the answer across from the new Anchorage building, where the logs that floated by the conference grounds had lodged themselves solidly against the bank of the property nearest the creek.

These massive logs protected the conference grounds from mountains of debris, which had floated up the creek and landed on neighboring property. In addition, the logs prevented the lumber, which they had stored near the creek, from floating back down the river as the water receded. The logs had kept the lumber safe.

The water, which carried with it large quantities of silt, had left sediment behind, filling in the very low ground on the creek end of the conference center. While God protected the property, at the same time He managed to bring in more fill dirt than the conference center could afford to purchase on its own.

Even in disaster, God managed the impossible.

Extensive water damage, experienced all over Cannon Beach, changed the city's policy on construction safety; the city required new buildings to be built above a new, higher, high-water mark. For the conference center, this regulation forced the second phase of the new lodge—where the new registration area, lobby, snack bar, and bookstore would be located—to be elevated two full steps above the first phase.

Those volunteers building the second phase worried that the height difference would distract observers. Certainly people would wonder about this strange "misplanning" of elevation. They would never know that these two strange steps were the unavoidable result of an earthquake whose epicenter was more than 1,500 miles away.

The second phase would also house a second floor meeting room, seating about 200 people. Evangeline had always dreamed about having another location to hold smaller gatherings during the off-season. The smaller room would have better lighting than the chapel and be easier to heat in the winter. Its unusual shape encouraged the placement of a small platform overlooking the south lawn.

<hr/>

The second meeting room had large windows and sliding glass doors, which led to a wide wrap-around porch. This new room could be accessed from the second floor guest wings on both sides of the building.

When the time came to build the second phase, Evangeline assembled her reliable crew of volunteer help. The unusual wedge shape of the new building demanded that every floor and ceiling joist be hand cut to exacting angles. Even her most committed volunteers refused to make these cuts.

Evangeline called the building's designer in Seattle. "Gordon, do you think you and Emmet Peterson could come down and help us? Not a carpenter who comes to the conference will touch those beams. They're afraid."

"Evangeline, do you mean the designer has to come down and erect all those beams in self-defense?" Gordon laughed.

"Well," she said, "it rather looks that way."

Of course Gordon and Emmet would help. Immediately they packed their cars and said good-bye to their families. As she kissed her husband, Austa Nickell asked with a chuckle, "Is there anything you won't do for that red-headed widow?"

"Now, dear Austa," Gordon answered back, "how much help do you think she would get if she weren't such a charming and beautiful red-headed widow?"

At the conference grounds, Emmet and Gordon carefully cut and erected each beam, pair by pair until finally all the hips and valleys of the roof were in place.

"Well you did it!" Evangeline exclaimed happily.

"Of course we did," Gordon replied. "Simple geometry—nothing more. And not only are all those beams in place, we did it without running out of timbers. We came out exactly right—we didn't cut any of the beams twice."

Evangeline shrugged. "Oh, well, you ordered them didn't you?"

"Yes, I did," he replied.

"Well, then you should have been right!"

Volunteers completed the second phase of the new building by the next summer season. As usual, Evangeline managed to save money as she supervised the project. She bought the carpet at a bargain price—from the platform of a Billy Graham crusade held in Portland. "Why it's as good as new!" she exclaimed.

When the time came to put in light fixtures, she asked Gordon what he had in mind. "Well," he replied, "I was thinking of 16-inch globes."

As Evangeline drove to Portland to look for globes, she prayed over her mission. It did not surprise Evangeline when the lighting man told her that 16-inch globes were not in demand at all any more. "In fact, they're a burden for me to store. I'll give them to you for less than I paid for them."

By 1967, the third and final stage of the buildings which became East and North Haven was complete. Conference attendance continued to climb. Evangeline's conference schedule expanded to include eight spring and four fall events. These off-season conferences were her biggest challenge as she had difficulty finding staff for a single isolated weekend.

She managed by asking college students to come and work at the beach; the students brought friends. By working very hard for the weekend, students managed to earn a little extra money and have some free time to enjoy the beach. But planning these off-season conferences required that Evangeline spend the winter in Oregon. So, while she continued to start Clubs and Council groups for the Christian Women's Club, she no longer did it from Stonecroft.

In many ways, life had changed for Evangeline. Heather had graduated from college, and after teaching school for some time, began work in Washington D.C. Helen Jean had nearly grown up. Having adult daughters enabled Evangeline to focus all her energy on traveling, speaking, and of course, on the ministry of the conference center.

As the sixties drew to a close, Evangeline reflected on the amazing things the Lord had accomplished. The conference center ministry was thriving. She frequently hosted such nationally known speakers as Dr. J. Vernon McGee, Dr. Allen Redpath, and Reverend John Hunter. These men, together with modern accommodations and the outstanding location of the conference center, had thrust the ministry into a decade of growth.

When they began, she and Archie had planned to minister extensively to young people. But God seemed to have changed her course. Now, she ministered mainly to adults and families. The old hotel was no longer a camp; it had become a resort. Somehow, God had moved Evangeline into a new ministry without her even realizing it had happened.

CHAPTER FIFTEEN

Ecola Hall

During the sixties, the conference center at Cannon Beach experienced incredible growth. In 10 years, Evangeline had led the construction of three major building projects. She had developed both a full-time staff, and the procedures which guided conference center operations. Attendance at summer conferences soared; the new buildings were consistently filled.

For the rest of the world, the sixties had been a decade of unrest. Besides the war in Vietnam, there was violence at home, on college campuses, and on city streets. In the midst of the sexual revolution, drug use exploded. Violence on the streets included the assassination of pastors, presidents, and senators.

For most ordinary women, the successes Evangeline experienced during the previous decade might have been enough. But in 1971, at 67 years of age, Evangeline McNeill had no desire to slow down.

She felt that cultural change had also occurred inside the church. The decade of the 60s found liberalism firmly entrenched in many mainline churches. Evangelical churches, while maintaining their connection to biblical truth, fell into complacency.

While they had the truth, evangelical churches did little to respond to the cultural war going on around them. Evangeline, keenly aware of her culture, recognized the dissatisfaction of young people in the United States. She understood their frustration with the answers being offered by the older generation. The demonstrations and violence were only a symptom of that dissatisfaction.

As this new generation turned its back on every tie to the traditions held sacred by their parents, Evangeline's long-standing concern for young people rose to the surface. She could not help but notice the young people who accidentally wandered onto the conference grounds looking for lodging.

Many of these inadvertent guests wore the trappings of their culture. They were the beatnik generation—longhaired, unclean, speaking a language all their own. But their appearance did not concern Evangeline. She seized every opportunity to share with them the good news about her Savior. Often she stopped to pray with those passing by. If she could meet a need, she did. If not, she would be on her way.

Strangers often watched her go, shaking their heads in wonder.

As her concern grew, Evangeline wanted desperately to reach the young people who wandered up and down the Pacific Coast in droves. So when a young Portland couple came to her with a plan, she listened.

The couple's plan involved using the old "Cannon Beach Recreation Center" building, which still stood on the beachfront property she had purchased in 1957. The conference center used the upper floor for staff housing; but the lower floor, which included two storefronts accessible to the street, remained vacant. The couple hoped to turn one of these storefronts into a coffee house ministry. Here, they would try to reach young people with the gospel.

Evangeline planned to demolish the old building and build a replacement as soon as she could arrange the plans and materials. But until then, she reasoned, the property might have some eternal function. So with her blessing, the couple cleaned and decorated one of the storefronts and opened it as an outreach for young people.

Though the coffee house ministry was a start, it didn't satisfy Evangeline's concern for her culture. But she was not the only one concerned.

David Duff, Evangeline's nephew and Walter Duff's youngest son, also recognized the empty and aimless lives of the young people around him. Having grown up in a Christian home, where Christian values were clearly demonstrated in his everyday life, his memories revolved around times spent at the conference center. It was there he made his first commitment to Christ. And there, seven years later, he first felt the call to Christian ministry.

From early adolescence through his first three years of college, David Duff worked at the conference center every summer. Having worked in every building, at nearly every job, the conference center became his home away from home. He considered his aunt Evangeline his "summer mom."

Though David knew he'd been called to full-time Christian work, he did not know where or to whom he would minister. Thinking about these questions, David knew he needed further training. He decided to attend Capernwray Hall, in Lancashire, Northern England. Located in an old English country home, the school had about 200 students living in dormitories on the school grounds. Teachers were guest lecturers, who came for one or two weeks of teaching.

Here, David became grounded in the systematic study and application of the Bible. Though he had been exposed, as a child, to some of the most prominent Christian speakers of his day, he had not understood the Bible in a personal, methodical way. His time at Capernwray Hall was a life-changing experience.

While at school in England, David spent his three-week Christmas break in London where he stayed in an unoccupied flat. As David walked the London streets, the faces of people he met distressed him. The young people seemed downcast, without hope. The English youth spent much of their time in the pubs. There were few jobs, and any extra money went for after-work drinks. Their hopelessness haunted David.

He began to wonder if the Lord were speaking to him. As he spent time praying about his experience, the thought occurred to him. Why not have schools like Capernwray in the United States? For that matter, why not have a whole string of them? Through the rest of the school term, the Lord continued to impress David with this need.

When he returned to Oregon, he waited for just the right moment to share his idea with his family. By midsummer, David had spoken about the possibility of a school with his parents, and his aunts Helen Baugh and Evangeline McNeill.

His idea made sense to them.

In the United States, the Jesus movement brought great waves of young people to Christ. Few of these new believers had any means of growing in their new faith. David's family recognized that such a school would serve to disciple these young believers, to train them in the Bible and anchor their faith. With their enthusiastic support and encouragement, David invited a board to gather and consider the possibility of starting a short-term, non-accredited Bible school on the campus of Cannon Beach Christian Conference Center.

At the board meeting, David emphasized how many of the needed arrangements were already in place. Because conference center facilities were completely unused during the winter months, they could easily house both the school and the students. Through the conference center, they could easily make contacts for visiting instructors. Between Village Missions, Christian Women's Councils and Clubs, and the conference center, they had a ready-made avenue for publicity.

Evangeline McNeill was thrilled to serve on the board of the new school. She and Archie had always dreamed that some kind of Christian school would occupy the conference grounds. Though she had no experience, Evangeline trusted David. Her instinct told her that more than ever, the young people of this generation needed all the training they could get to live the Christian life successfully.

David's school provided another answer to her growing concern for the strange young people she met on the streets and beaches of Cannon Beach.

Evangeline gave David her full support. Before the conference center could house the school, it needed much work. Most of the buildings had not been used in winter; so Evangeline began by installing heating systems and insulation. The dining hall's second floor, where they hoped to house students, consisted of family-style rooms with double beds and no study areas. She had the double beds removed and bunks installed, carpets laid, and the rooms painted. They added new circuits to provide electricity to each room. They also renovated the boy's dorm, on the second floor of the administration building, to provide additional student housing.

While they hammered and painted, the nearby Gearhart Hotel closed, offering all its furniture and fixtures for sale. Evangeline and David made many trips to the hotel to purchase furniture. Clearly, the woman in charge of the sale liked David. For Evangeline, her prices were stiff. But for David, invariably, her prices went down.

Together, David and Evangeline obtained old carpets, old oak dressers, matching headboards and mirrors, restaurant chairs, and even a used ice machine.

As Evangeline prepared the buildings, David began to advertise its opening. His cousin, Gordon Baugh, enthusiastically agreed to contact and schedule the school's speakers. David contacted another cousin, Heather McNeill, who was working in the Washington D.C. area. He asked her to be the school's full-time secretary. She agreed, and moved back to Cannon Beach.

Evangeline hired a cook, and found someone to supervise the food service for the winter months. Then she made arrangements for a winter maintenance man.

That first year, while leaning over a counter in the conference administration building, David and Evangeline determined tuition. If tuition were too high, they reasoned, they would have no students. More than anything, they wanted the school to succeed. So they set the first year's tuition at $660 for three, eight-week terms—including room and board. It was a bargain they would never repeat.

Gordon Baugh agreed to serve as Dean of the new school. His academic background would contribute to the school's credibility. Gordon would supervise finances, curriculum, speaker arrangements, student admissions, and discipline.

David Duff would act as director of the school. Because he was gifted and comfortable speaking in front of people, he took responsibility for publicity, promotion, and student outreach. David would manage the daily program and also serve as chaplain.

Applications began to arrive. Students were eager to attend. This was, to all of them, another confirmation of the Lord's leading. In every turn, He seemed to be moving ahead of them. Remarkably, the school opened 14 months after David shared his dream.

Surprisingly, Evangeline discovered another unexpected benefit from locating the school on the conference grounds.

She had long wished for the grounds to be used during the winter; but many factors prevented her dream from coming true. In the winter, many of the conference buildings were locked up, the water turned off, the oil drained. She found it impractical to close the buildings, reopen them for a weekend conference or two, and then close them up again.

In order to make financial ends meet, Mrs. McNeill continued to travel through winter months for Christian Women's Clubs and Councils. While away from the grounds, she found it difficult to keep her travel and speaking commitments and at the same time supervise a retreat schedule for the conference center.

Perhaps the most serious difficulty in using the grounds through the winter had to do with staff. Having scheduled weekend couples conferences every fall and spring, Evangeline found it nearly impossible to find enough staff to clean, cook, and serve so many guests.

The Bible school's presence on campus changed all that. Now, there were people on campus who could supervise meals, facilities and maintenance. She found herself with many students who needed financial help to pay for Bible school. They became willing workers who cleaned rooms, served meals, and helped with facilities while attending school.

With the Bible school in session, the conference center could provide retreat facilities for private groups of all sizes and denominations throughout the entire winter season. With these advantages in mind, Mrs. McNeill chose to stay at Cannon Beach during the winter to help supervise what quickly became a year-round operation. The unexpected and wonderful side effects of having a school on the conference grounds delighted Evangeline.

CHAPTER SIXTEEN

Passing the Torch

*T*hough Evangeline looked forward to the growth and development of the Ecola Hall Bible School, she had other dreams as well. Her driving desire was to plan and construct a building on the old Recreation Center property. For some time, Evangeline did not know what she would build—a new dining hall? A new meeting area? After much thought and prayer, and after consultation with the city of Cannon Beach, she decided to build another guest building.

She dreamed of a building that would include a large second-floor meeting room overlooking the ocean. Directly below this room, the building would have a smaller dining hall and kitchen. It would house 20 guest rooms, 12 facing west toward the ocean and eight overlooking the north beach and Ecola State Park.

Because the building location forced guests to cross two busy intersections as they walked to the conference grounds, Evangeline planned it to function as an "adults only" building. Evangeline believed the project would take several years to complete.

Before new construction could begin, Evangeline would have to remove the existing Rec Center building. Of course she did not destroy the old building until every scrap of usable material had been salvaged. Volunteers removed and stored every window, every door, every plumbing fixture, all the extra wood, and any little item they might someday use.

Then demolition began. After tying a cable around the center of the building the crew increased tension until the wire actually cut the building in half and the building fell in on itself.

Next, because the western border of the Recreation Center property lay directly against the winter high water line, they would have to build a mammoth seawall. Without it, raging storms and winter high tides would threaten the new building.

Though she knew nothing about such a task, Evangeline had Gordon Nickell draw the plans. She did not expect her regular volunteers to safely build such a giant seawall. Evangeline needed a professional. Because she did not know anyone with this kind of expertise, and could not afford to hire anyone, she began, as usual, to pray.

On the other side of the country, Warren Goss and his family planned their summer vacation. They hoped to make a cross-country car trip from their home in Pittsburgh to the Pacific Coast, beginning with a visit to Helen Baugh at Stonecroft.

Early the next summer, the Goss family left the hot, sultry East Coast behind. While visiting Helen, they found Missouri plagued by tornadoes. So they headed for southern California. There, to their discouragement, they had to pay a tow truck to remove their family car from the sand at Pismo Beach.

It was not the vacation they dreamed about!

The Goss family decided to visit Yosemite National Park—where they ran straight into a forest fire. After much adversity, and no small amount of consternation, the Goss family arrived quite unexpectedly at the Cannon Beach Christian Conference Center. There they enjoyed the cool coastal weather and the fine speaker scheduled for the week. At last, events had begun to break their way.

That is, until Mrs. Evangeline McNeill stood up to introduce the evening speaker in a chapel service. Almost casually, she mentioned that she had been praying for the Lord to bring a man to Cannon Beach who knew how to build a seawall. That was the last announcement Warren Goss wanted to hear. After all, he hadn't driven his family across the country to go back to work; this was vacation.

But he could not erase her comment from his mind.

Warren Goss owned a construction company that specialized in river walls. When he introduced himself to Mrs. McNeill, she asked him, "Could you build us a seawall?"

"I never have. But I could if I wanted to," he replied. "But I won't."

Warren could not resist Evangeline McNeill for long. Because of her enthusiasm and faith, he agreed to speak to the designer about the plans. Evangeline called Gordon.

But Gordon Nickell had left Seattle to attend a wedding in California. Though she tried numerous times to call, she missed him along the way. Warren Goss planned to leave soon. If Evangeline couldn't contact Gordon, the seawall would not be built. Helen Baugh, who had come to the coast to visit Evangeline, agreed that it was time to pray. And pray they did.

That evening, when the dinner bell rang, who should enter the dining room but designer Gordon Nickell? Helen greeted him warmly. "Imagine seeing you here," she said. "We've called three states to find you. Where have you been?"

"Well now, have you?" Gordon chuckled. "What do you need me for?"

"There is a man here from Pittsburgh who can build our sea wall. He wants desperately to talk to you. We wanted you to drive down and speak with him."

"So, that explains it," Gordon said, chuckling. "Just today, on our trip north, when we came to the 'Y' in the road where the coast highway meets the freeway, I felt strongly that we should come by Cannon Beach. If you and Evangeline prayed, it's no wonder I'm here."

After dinner Warren asked Gordon numerous technical questions. Less than an hour later, Gordon and his wife Austa headed home to Seattle, and Warren Goss made the decision to build his first seawall.

After studying the plans, he made a materials list and went to Portland to order the steel reinforcing rods. He rented a backhoe to do the trenching. He flew part of his crew out to the coast from Pennsylvania. Then Warren recruited willing volunteers from the conference center. Together, right on the new property, they built and oiled the forms for the concrete. Next they poured the seawall; the concrete began to flow at 8 A.M. By 3 p.m the crew had finished.

Warren recognized the scope of the miracle he'd witnessed. "You know honey," he said to his wife on the night the last of the forms were removed, "back home a project this size would have taken two months to complete. Here we finished in exactly six days. Only God could have done this."

"I know," she replied. "I've been thinking the same thing myself—how God used all those awful circumstances to bring us here. How we resisted the idea of building a seawall. You know, Warren, in all our wanderings, I've never felt so unquestionably used by God."

"Me, too," he replied. "It's so powerful, it's almost scary."

⌑

Later that summer, at the Sunday service of the local Presbyterian church, Evangeline noticed a young man sitting alone. *He looks lonely*, she thought. After the service, she invited him to join her for dinner at the conference center. "There are lots of young people there," she said. "You'll enjoy yourself."

Steve agreed. Later, at her home, Evangeline probed gently, wondering what had brought this young man to Cannon Bach from his home in California. She discovered that he had planned a trip to Alaska, driving north until he ran out of funds. Then Steve had located a temporary job and worked until he could afford to move on.

When Steve arrived at Cannon Beach, he found a construction project and asked the foreman if he could work for half the going wage. Steve was hired on the spot. As Evangeline listened to his story, she sensed his need for spiritual help. Later that summer she noticed Steve attending one or two of the conference sessions. Then, in the first part of August, he came to say good-bye. His had finished his job and would move on.

Concerned, Evangeline spoke up. "Perhaps you would consider staying on here. We're starting a new building project this fall and we could use an experienced carpenter."

Steve considered her offer.

Evangeline did not know everything about him. She could not know that he drank heavily. That earlier his drinking had caused a serious car accident. That as Steve lay in the hospital, struggling with pain, God had begun to speak to him. Steve sensed God in Evangeline's offer. He accepted, happy for an excuse to stay near the conference center.

God's provision for what became the Beachfront building continued. Because Evangeline planned to start construction during "work week" in the fall of 1972, she began considering her need for lumber. Her old friend George Miller had retired from the lumber business.

Evangeline went to see his son, Bud Miller, who ran the mill in his father's place, and showed him the materials list. Though he was polite, he did not promise the lumber. Instead, he asked for a copy of the list, and sent her on her way.

Several days later Evangeline noticed a letter from Bud Miller in her mail. Quickly she scanned it. "I would be glad to sell half of your lumber to you at wholesale prices," he began. Disappointed, Evangeline continued reading. "The remainder I would like to give you as our personal gift to the conference center."

Evangeline laughed. God continued to provide.

A builder from Spokane volunteered to get the new building underway. During the first week, his skill, his power nailer and power equipment gave the building a good start. When he returned to Spokane, Steve continued as best he could, but Evangeline knew that he needed more experienced help. She prayed. Then she received a phone call from a carpenter who was out of work. "Could you use some help?" he asked. Mike McIntyre joined the project.

This new guest unit was the largest, most complicated building the conference center had yet constructed. Mike needed advice from someone with more experience. But there was no one on campus to give construction advice. Again they prayed.

Then, Ecola Hall—the new short-term non-accredited Bible school—received a most interesting letter. A Canadian woman wrote to the school: "I would like very much to go to Ecola Hall. Do you take older people? Incidentally, my husband, who is a contractor, and I frequently leave Canada for a winter holiday. Would you have any use for his ability?"

Needless to say, Evangeline had much use for a contractor.

As work on the Beachfront building progressed, God seemed to anticipate their every need. Though Evangeline was nearly 70 years old, she continued to oversee every detail of the construction. She became aware of a new technology that used light concrete to dampen sound traveling from floor to floor. Determined to add this advantage to the new building, Evangeline contacted local companies to obtain the correct materials. No one handled it. Worried that bringing the concrete in from Portland would add astronomical costs to her project, Evangeline pondered the question. Then she remembered a nearby family who attended summer conferences. She seemed to remember that their business had something to do with light rock. She called them.

Mr. Schultz answered the phone himself. "Of course I understand, Mrs. McNeill. I know exactly what you need. Why don't I come to see you when I am up in Cannon Beach this weekend?"

On the construction site, Mr. Schultz carefully examined the building. "Mrs. McNeill," he said, "it's the only way to go. It will definitely quiet the building; but it's very costly."

Disappointed, Evangeline said, "Well, if it's costly, we'll just have to forget it. We can't handle any added expense."

"Oh, no, Mrs. McNeill," Schultz objected. "The concrete will be a gift from us to the conference center."

In January of 1973, one of the Ecola Hall outreach teams presented music in the Grays Harbor area of the Washington coast. After their program, they spoke to the audience about all the happenings at the Cannon Beach Christian Conference Center.

Hearing about the new building project, a subcontractor came forward. "Is there any possibility that you would need a concrete finisher? I am out of work most of January. If you need help in my line, I would be glad to come now."

God provided the concrete *and* the concrete finisher.

Steve, the transient carpenter, continued work on the Beachfront building. He showed initiative and commitment. He was also fascinated by the presence of the Bible school on the grounds. Later that winter, he came to Mrs. McNeill. "You know, Mrs. McNeill, I am building over there on the beach. But, my heart is over here at the Bible school. I need to be in Bible school."

Steve enrolled as a full-time student the next term.

When it came time to choose windows, Evangeline did as much research as she could. She learned that salt water and winter storms cause serious damage to windows on the coast. With the new building directly above the winter surf line, she needed a window which would endure the blustery coast conditions.

All of her research pointed to one particular brand, which naturally, was the most expensive brand on the market. But, if any window would hold up under rugged beach conditions, the Viking would manage. Desperate to obtain the windows at a reasonable cost, Evangeline tried all of her connections. Nothing turned up.

One morning in the middle of a couples conference weekend, Evangeline spent her entire prayer time on the need for windows. After the morning session, a man introduced himself to Evangeline as a lumber broker.

"If you need materials," he said, "I may be able to get them for you at considerable savings." Evangeline thanked him warmly. But lumber she already had. She needed windows.

Some weeks later, Evangeline spoke to the broker again by phone. Suddenly it occurred to her to ask, "Do you have any contacts for windows?"

"I can only get one type of window," he said. "A Viking."

Lumber. Concrete. Windows. Evangeline gratefully received all that God provided.

Considered a bird-dog for bargains, those around her knew that whenever there was a batch of anything with little imperfections, Evangeline knew where it was and how to obtain it. When the new building needed carpet, she scouted for the best buy, asking every supplier, "Haven't you anything for less than that?"

At last a carpet salesman replied, "Well, yes, we have. But it's all red."

"Wonderful," she replied, eyes twinkling. "That is exactly the color we want."

And so Evangeline found carpet for exactly $1.25 per yard. Though the carpet had some factory imperfections, the men who installed it cut around them quite nicely.

Many women had made reservations to stay in the new building for the Women's World conference of May 1973. Though nearly completed, Evangeline stayed up most of the night to finish painting the hallway. If women had looked carefully, they would have noticed the paint was wet when they arrived.

To Evangeline, the Beachfront building represented tangible evidence of God's faithfulness toward the conference center ministry. Evangeline could not look at it, or stand in the new hallway, or view His mighty creation from the new lounge, without feeling God's presence. She sensed His pleasure in providing for His children, in answering their prayer, in meeting their needs. The new building's completion left Evangeline with an overwhelming sense of praise.

The conference center's continuing growth kept Evangeline from focusing on past success. With Ecola Hall on campus the conference center experienced many changes. Perhaps the most significant was Heather McNeill's return to Cannon Beach. Though she came to help the new Bible school, Evangeline quickly realized that she needed Heather more than David Duff or Ecola Hall.

With everyone's agreement, Heather became her mother's new assistant.

Mother and daughter worked well together. Heather managed the conference center and supervised the winter guest retreats while Evangeline traveled with her speaking engagements. Heather did the daily cash reports. As Evangeline trained her daughter, she freely shared her wisdom and insight into the ministry.

Shortly after the Beachfront was finished, Evangeline received a call from an older woman who lived directly across the city park from the new Beachfront Lodge. The woman wanted to talk to Evangeline. Would Evangeline and Heather please come for tea the following afternoon?

Her request puzzled them. Though they knew the woman—she was a long-time Cannon Beach resident—they had no idea what she could want to talk about. They hoped that their latest building project hadn't offended her.

When Evangeline and Heather arrived, the woman received them warmly and seated them in her parlor. While they enjoyed the ocean view, Mrs. Becker served hot tea and delicious cookies. Before long, she shared her story with the McNeills.

Mrs. Becker told them her husband's family had purchased five oceanfront lots at the turn of the century, building their first little cottage in 1904. In the seventy years since, they had added two more houses.

When her children were small, Mrs. Becker brought them to Cannon Beach for summer vacations. They came by buckboard from Portland to Seaside along the Columbia River. Then they proceeded along the coast to Cannon Beach. Over the years, her family had spent many happy days at the beach.

Mrs. Becker's husband, a contractor, had died leaving her very wealthy. She needed nothing. "Over the past years, I have been watching your work very carefully. I like you. I like the kind of people you bring to Cannon Beach. Quality people. I like the way you take care of the things you own. You are my kind of people.

"My children and I have decided to sell this property. We have an offer of $150,000 from one of our neighbors. But, we would like for you to have it. I would be willing to sell to you for $125,000. As I said, we would rather you have it. Please consider my offer, Mrs. McNeill."

The proposal flabbergasted Evangeline. Having just finished a major project, she had not considered buying additional property. Evangeline explained her obligation to pray about the matter. "I wouldn't want to make a mistake," she said. "I will give the matter much prayer and thought."

Heather had been relatively quiet during the whole visit. As they walked home, she asked her mother, "What do you think?"

"I think that until now, I had no plans to buy property. But who knows what God may be doing? It certainly is an unusual situation. I'll call all of the board members and ask for their counsel. Then I will do as I explained; I will pray."

The next morning, Evangeline woke with a light heart. When Heather saw her mother, she asked, "What have you decided?"

Evangeline explained, "I have decided to offer the woman $80,000."

"But Mother, she will be insulted! That isn't what she suggested."

"Well, you may be right. But we know she has a much better offer. She can always accept that. On the other hand, if she takes our offer, we will know without a doubt that God wants us to have it."

Evangeline arranged to visit Mrs. Becker in her Portland home. When she arrived at the elegant, expensive home, a butler greeted her at the door and escorted her to a living room. Evangeline explained her situation to Mrs. Becker.

"I hope you don't take offense at our offer. It is just that we had no intention of buying more property. And, in truth, we don't have anything saved to pay for this. But if you will accept my offer of $80,000, I will know that this is God's plan. I will expect Him to provide the money as well."

Graciously, Mrs. Becker escorted Evangeline to the door promising to consider the proposal. A few weeks later, Mrs. Becker told Evangeline that she and her children would be happy to sell the land and buildings to the conference center for $80,000.

Owning this new piece of property enabled Evangeline to start yet another conference center ministry. In 1974, a young couple approached her with the idea of starting a youth hostel. The hostel would provide Cannon Beach some much needed relief from the waves of poor young people traveling through town. With little money, they tended to camp in any location—the beach, local parks and picnic benches in the center of town. Local businesses considered the young people a serious nuisance.

With the approval of the conference board, Evangeline opened a Youth Hostel in one of Mrs. Becker's homes at the north end of town. The townspeople loved getting the campers off the public streets. Evangeline was delighted to have another opportunity to expose these young travelers to the gospel. During the first year, the hostel provided housing for more than thirteen hundred youths. Many of these made first time decisions for Christ. Every guest heard the gospel and had an opportunity to respond.

Evangeline's life consisted of more than construction and new ministries. She also had the joy of seeing both her daughters married. On August 7, 1971, Helen Jean married Charles Steynor, of Bermuda. Charles, a ruddy-faced blond, had a charming Bermudian accent. His experience in the hospitality business was an asset to his work at the conference center. Together Charles and Helen Jean presented Evangeline with her first grandchild, Andrew Steynor, born on December 16, 1973.

Evangeline became a devoted grandmother. She loved to play on the beach and to roughhouse with the young boy. Because she had begun traveling less, she had more time to spend with Andrew.

Just two years later, her oldest daughter, Heather, married Dale Goodenough. Dale had come to the conference center as an Ecola Hall student and stayed to join the conference center staff. His practical ability with mechanical things made him a much-valued addition to the conference family.

Evangeline had seen so much in ten years—the building of Beachfront Lodge, the purchase of new property, the marriage of her girls.

In the midst of constant upkeep, building projects, management of staff, and the joy of her growing family, Evangeline also discovered the potential for off-season guest retreats. Unwilling to settle for things as they were, Evangeline, now 71, pushed full steam ahead.

Chapter Seventeen

The Home Stretch

*A*s the 1976 summer season drew to a close, Heather grew concerned about her mother's health. While Evangeline completed all her usual duties, she seemed to lack her usual zest for life. The staff noticed that her plates often went back to the kitchen untouched. Occasionally, she complained of "stomach problems." After much urging, Evangeline consented to see a doctor.

The Rinehart Clinic in Wheeler, Oregon, agreed that something was wrong. However, lab results were not definitive. Mrs. McNeill would need more tests.

Evangeline believed that rest and sunshine would replenish her health. "I've been asked to speak in Santa Barbara," she told Heather. "It will be the perfect 'pick me up.' You'll see. When I return, I'll be my old self."

Heather knew better than to try to change her mother's mind. Part of her hoped that Evangeline was right. Having just finished a long conference season, perhaps extra rest would help. At any rate, Evangeline would travel with her close friends Faye Southard and Rosemary Reed. Certainly Rosemary, a registered nurse, could take excellent care of her mother. Reluctantly, Heather sent Evangeline to California.

Only a week after their departure, Faye called Heather. Evangeline had become desperately sick. Rosemary believed that she needed to see a doctor.

They made arrangements to fly Evangeline to Seattle, where her brother Haldane would take her to visit his own physician. Dr. Fred Hutchinson, a very capable specialist, would certainly get to the bottom of her illness.

Evangeline's condition alarmed Dr. Hutchinson. He admitted her to Swedish Hospital for several days of testing. Evangeline had a blockage in her colon. She would need surgery.

Walter and Edith joined Haldane and Ethel in Seattle. Walter was relieved when he saw Evangeline. Though she was thinner than she had ever been, she still wanted to be "in charge."

Her surgery took several hours. When Dr. Hutchinson met with the family, he told them that Evangeline was filled with inoperable cancer.

Nothing prepared Walter for the broken-hearted sister he greeted after surgery. "Walter, it's cancer," she said simply and wept.

Walter understood her grief. Evangeline had so much left to do. So many more things to accomplish. She had no time for illness, much less death. Evangeline McNeill had always hoped she would live to see the Lord's return.

In a few days, the old confident Evangeline was back. When her brothers visited the hospital, the three of them went for long walks down hospital corridors. They spent hours planning strategies for her recovery. Days later, she was discharged to Haldane's home where she spent another week resting. Then, just before Thanksgiving, she went to Walter's home in Dallas, Oregon.

There they enjoyed an unseasonably warm fall, allowing Evangeline to sit for long hours in a sheltered corner of the yard absorbing sunshine and fresh air. As her strength returned, she began to take walks. She planned her trips so that she could rest on park benches and stop at the fabric store to rest at the pattern counter. Then she would begin the long, slow trek back to Walter's home.

Religiously, she followed the treatment and diet prescribed for her. Color returned to her cheeks and she began to gain weight. Life began to feel good again. Hope arose in their hearts. Perhaps Evangeline would defeat this evil disease.

While she recovered, her children worked furiously to keep the conference center going. Every week, Heather drove to Dallas to visit her mother. During their long talks, Evangeline gave Heather instructions for the staff. Even as Evangeline fought cancer, she continued to worry over conference center details.

Because of her busy life, Evangeline had never learned to enjoy television; but now, forced to rest, she discovered that she enjoyed Masterpiece Theater. It was so British. Walter once discovered Evangeline, snuggled under a blanket in his favorite recliner, watching "Upstairs Downstairs."

Though forced to rest, the conference center was always on her mind. As soon as she felt able, she directed the staff by telephone. Walter found her in the kitchen nearly every morning, impeccably dressed, making phone calls. From Dallas, she planned the conference program, contacted musicians and speakers, and made arrangements for the coming season.

Evangeline—a very private person—requested that no one reveal her illness to the public. Walter suspected that she felt some shame in having cancer—especially during the rise of the "faith movement." More likely, he thought, Evangeline simply had no intention of dying. She had little patience with the long condolence letters she received. She fully intended to beat her disease.

Evangeline would not die; she had too much left to do.

Barbara Cole, Evangeline's close friend approached the cancer diagnosis differently. In 1973 Barbara had her own brush with cancer. Surgery gave Barbara life. Over the next years, Barbara often testified about how God sustained her during her own brush with death.

Though young enough to be Evangeline's daughter, the two women had developed an abiding friendship. Barbara, having played the organ at the conference center for years, greatly respected Evangeline. She believed that Evangeline showed all women what God could do with a fully devoted heart.

Barbara heard about Evangeline's illness from another friend on the conference center staff. She knew Evangeline wanted privacy. Evangeline, the spiritual giant, had set her course. Yet, Barbara couldn't quite let the issue go. Could she have something important to say to Evangeline? Risking their friendship, Barbara decided to write.

When Evangeline discovered Barbara's letter in the mail, she was not happy. Another letter of sympathy, she thought. But the words and sentiment Barbara expressed surprised Evangeline.

"Okay kiddo, so you have cancer," it began. "Well, of course we all want you to live a long and healthy life. We are not ready to give up on you. We love you. But we do have to remember that God is in this. What is His timing? Really, cancer isn't so bad. God will help you live with it or die with it. He has helped me so far. And I know, with certainty, that He will help you. I want you to know that I understand what you are going through. I know too that you are keeping the facts from others. But I also know from experience that if you are willing to share with others and be open, you can receive a lot of comfort and healing from people.

"You know, Evangeline, you have been a blessing in my life. When I had cancer, you were there to encourage and care for me. I can never thank you enough for the many prayers you offered on my behalf. I do thank you.

"Please, Evangeline, don't deny others the privilege of caring for you—just as you have cared for others."

Later when Barbara learned that her letter had made a great deal of difference to Evangeline, she couldn't have been more pleased. Of course, Evangeline thanked her; but she did more. As a result of Barbara's letter, Evangeline began to risk telling people about her illness.

During the day, Evangeline experienced minimal pain. But the nights were not so pleasant. Because she suffered constant nausea, she got up at all hours of the night to eat small bits of food. Sleep was elusive. Ever the caring brother, Walter often rose with Evangeline during the night. Sometimes he prepared oatmeal. Often, he simply stayed with her until the nausea subsided enough to allow sleep.

By Christmas, Evangeline felt well enough to long for a family visit. "If only everyone could be together again," she said. "How I would love to have everyone spend Christmas together at my house on the coast."

Walter called Olive in California, and Helen in Missouri. Haldane agreed to come from Seattle. Together, the Duffs would make her wish come true.

Evangeline enjoyed a wonderful Christmas in Cannon Beach. Her brothers and sisters talked about the old days. They took pictures. They sang. They laughed. Evangeline had recovered well; in fact she looked so lovely that her family found it hard to believe that she had not beat the cancer. She experienced Christmas of 1976 exactly as she had wished.

When Evangeline returned to Dallas with Walter and Edith, her health continued to improve. Their hopes rose higher still. Evangeline's family continued to drive to Dallas for visits.

As she recovered, the visits of her only grandchild—Helen Jean's son, Andrew—gave Evangeline overwhelming joy. Even in her weariness, he thrilled her. Often, when he came, she took the boy to her room, only to be discovered later crawling about on her hands and knees, playing "horsy" with him.

After Helen Jean left with Andrew, loneliness overtook her. Both Helen Jean and Heather lived in Cannon Beach.

Walter's home was too far away for frequent visits. "If only I knew I wasn't going to make it. I would want to spend my time at home, with my girls and with Andrew," she said.

Her longing grew into a request. Walter and Edith struggled with the decision. Her diet was very strict. Her medicine required constant supervision. How would Evangeline care for herself at home? Yet, they understood her desire to be near the people and things that comforted her most.

Reluctantly, they agreed to take her home to Cannon Beach. They hoped the decision would benefit everyone. The girls would be spared driving to Dallas in the winter weather. Walter and Edith could use the much-needed break to visit some Village missionaries in Arizona and Nevada.

Heather made arrangements for a woman to stay with Evangeline in her home and Evangeline returned to the coast she loved.

Three weeks later, when Walter and Edith returned from their trip, Evangeline called. They hardly recognized her voice. "I think I'd better come back," she said.

Again they made the trip to Cannon Beach. They were not prepared for the change in Evangeline. She had lost weight. Her strength was gone. Her color was bad.

Walter could not understand how his sister had lost so much ground. After some investigation, he discovered that when she arrived at the coast, Evangeline was not content to rest. She had thrown herself back into her work, hosting meetings in the chapel, and supervising every conference department. Methodically she had visited every building— the kitchen, the administrative offices and every guest lodge.

At first, Walter fumed. How could she throw away her hard-won progress? Why would she deliberately risk her health?

Then Walter realized—Evangeline was saying good-bye.

Still Walter would not give up; he would win back her remission. He and Edith brought her back to Dallas and started her on a new and more vigorous treatment program.

They made yet another trip to Seattle to visit her doctor. Sadly, he told them there was nothing left to do.

With this news, Evangeline—perhaps for the first time—recognized that she was nearing her own end. She entered into a gracious acceptance of things as they were. She was not terribly ill. They were grateful for that.

They returned to Dallas by plane.

Walter encouraged her to complete whatever things she felt she needed to finish. "I think we need to tell the story of the conference center," she said. "People need to know what has happened there. God has done such wonderful, impossible things. I want to tell them about it before I go."

With that she began to write. On the back of church bulletins, on old calendars, on scratch paper, Evangeline began to write. Over and over, she edited the work. Time and again she retold her favorite stories, each style having its own effect.

The writing gave Evangeline great pleasure.

Helen came to Dallas from Stonecroft to stay with her sister. Olive came from California, and Haldane from Seattle. The five siblings spent hours together in her room, reading her scratchings and reminiscing about the "old days." Together they recreated the details of their lives together—so interconnected, so related. Again Evangeline rewrote the latest version of her story, and together they critiqued the work.

Walter treasured the days; they were precious, wonderful hours. The Duff Evangelistic Team was together again.

The doctor in Dallas came to see her. Wanting to be home with her family, Evangeline refused to go to the hospital. Walter rented a hospital bed. The stream of family and friends coming to visit gave her great joy.

Evangeline delighted in one last precious gift. On May 11, 1977, her second grandchild, Erica, was born. Helen Jean often came to visit with the two children.

Others came as well. Evangeline's dear friend Mary Rice came bringing lamb—the only meat Evangeline was allowed to eat—for Walter's freezer. It was Mary's way of loving Evangeline. She always brought lamb.

As her strength began its final ebb, Evangeline made her last and most important request. During a visit from Heather and Dale she asked the others to leave the room. She began to speak from her heart.

"I am not going to last much longer," she began—

"Mother, please don't talk this way," Heather said and began to cry.

"I must," she insisted. "I love you Heather, you know that. And Dale, I feel as though you are my own son. I wouldn't speak this way unless it was very important to me. I want for you to take over the conference center. I trust you. I know you both understand the dream. Together you can guide it, shape it—but not destroy it. It is so important that this is settled before I die. Please. Promise that you will do this for me?"

With many tears, Heather and Dale promised. It was their last visit with Evangeline.

Evangeline slipped into death gently. In the presence of Walter and Helen, on June 16, 1977 at 11 A.M., she flew away. And Archie welcomed her home.

Epilogue

For 25 years, Evangeline McNeill managed Cannon Beach Christian Conference Center alone. During this time, she directed nine major building projects, along with innumerable renovations, upgrades and remodeling projects. The staff grew from a handful of volunteers to nearly 20 paid summer positions. The number of summer conferences increased from four in 1945, to ten in 1976. In addition, Evangeline added 17 conference weekends to the yearly schedule. At the time of her death in 1977, the mailing list contained 18,000 names. The private retreat business had begun to explode.

In Christian ministry, the death of an originator sometimes leads to the death of the ministry. Somehow, ministry loses momentum, memories fade, dreams die. Not so at Cannon Beach Christian Conference Center.

When Evangeline McNeill died, she left behind an army of people who continued to care about and carry on the ministry she began.

Her daughter, Heather McNeill Goodenough, assumed the position of Conference Director. With the help of her husband, Dale, her sister Helen Jean, and brother-in-law Charles Steynor, the Conference Center made it through the difficult loss of Evangeline Duff McNeill.

Heather Goodenough added her own unique qualities of leadership to her mother's work. Through the 60s and 70s, Heather had watched enormous growth force her mother to focus entirely on facility development. Evangeline did not have time to develop an administrative structure to support the enormous growth. She had no budget, no clearly outlined policies and procedures to manage the conference center staff. There were no regular communications with those who attended the Conference Center.

During her tenure, Heather strove to meet these administrative, "behind the scenes" needs. Unlike her mother, Heather felt uncomfortable speaking in front of groups. Still, she developed the skill to direct a conference session. Though people who attended the Conference Center during Heather's season as director did not observe much in the way of change, much happened to support the Center's extensive growth.

Through the counsel of a fellow Christian conference leader, in 1977 Heather hired a business manager. Chuck Davenport and Joe Noegel, his successor, did much to add administrative and financial order to a ministry that was growing 10 to 20 percent each year.

Until Heather, Evangeline had run the conference center from the confines of her own imagination. Heather felt the time had come to commit these ideas and procedures to paper.

In 1982, Heather hired Janet Kerns to develop a more extensive program for children and families. Janet wrote a special children's curriculum, and added significantly to the summer family activities. With much organizational talent, Janet eventually moved into the administration of the guest retreat ministry. On any winter weekend, there are now three or more private retreats happening on various parts of the CBCC campus. Over 125 private retreats are held yearly, with many more turned away for lack of space.

After hiring Janet, Heather brought Jeff Carlsen on board as full-time program director. He supervised programming, advertising and conference hosting. Jeff would ease Heather's responsibilities, and help Janet expand family outreach.

In 1983 Charles Steynor accepted an administrative position at a conference center in his native Bermuda; he and Helen Jean left Cannon Beach. While Heather missed his influence at the Conference Center, she continued on as conference director, aided by a solid administrative team.

Trained as an elementary school teacher, Heather found herself directing what had become one of the major Christian ministries in the Northwest. Believing that she needed to turn conference center operations over to a more experienced ministry leader, Heather encouraged the Board of Directors to hire Bob Stephens. In 1988, Bob became Cannon Beach Christian Conference Center's fourth executive director and the first non-family member to serve in that position.

Bob and his wife Doris had served on the staff of The Navigators for 37 years, directing works in Boston, England, California, and Colorado. He served as general manager of Glen Eyrie Conference Center in Colorado Springs before coming to Cannon Beach.

Bob hoped to strengthen and stabilize the conference center's financial base while building a stronger ministry to conference staff. During his tenure, Bob Stephens supervised the construction of the New Tides building, the remodel the 43-year-old kitchen/dining room, the renovation of many guest facilities and the construction of the new 32-room Pacific View Lodge—by far the most ambitious project ever attempted by the conference center. With Bob directing operations, Heather chose to focus on board leadership and guest relations.

When Bob Stephens retired in May of 1996, Jeff Carlsen became executive director. Under his direction volunteers constructed a new recreation center, (finished in 2004), which provides year-round gymnasium and exercise facilities as well as much needed classroom space. With the opening of the recreation building, the conference center began a new outreach to the community—providing after-school care for Cannon Beach children.

Jeff supervised the renovation of the original chapel, as well as continued upkeep and updating of the campus buildings. With the assistance of guests and volunteers, plans for growth continue to move forward. With the purchase of the 22-room Ecola Creek Lodge, a new hotel ministry has been added to the work. With God's help, the conference center hopes to build a new dining facility and looks forward to additional guest or staff buildings.

Though some things have changed over the years, other things have not.

At Cannon Beach Christian Conference Center, God still works in the lives of people. He continues to heal marriages, save souls, encourage, challenge, and mature believers. He continues to call ordinary men and women into full-time ministry. He continues to mend broken hearts.

These stories, which continue day in and day out at the conference center, could not be contained within the pages of a single book.

While considering this revised version of Evangeline's biography, I asked Jeff Carlsen why God chooses to work through the ministry at the conference center.

"I've asked myself the same question," Jeff said, leaning back in his chair. "I think there are many factors coming into play. Part of it has to do with our heritage. Evangeline and Archie founded the conference center on a foundation of prayer. That legacy has continued over the years. We *ask* God to work here. We cover every aspect of our work with prayer. Our supporters pray for us. Prayer covers everything. I think that explains a lot.

"But there is more. People come to the conference center with a sense of expectation. They believe that God will meet them here, and they come eager to hear Him speak. I think He is pleased to respond to people who genuinely seek Him.

"I think another factor is that our staff realizes that we're stewards of something much bigger than ourselves. We know the history of the conference center, and we sense that we are both connected with the past, and responsible for the future.

"The conference center ministry is something that God has entrusted to us. We take that responsibility very seriously."

Since Evangeline McNeill's death, Cannon Beach Conference Center has experienced remarkable growth. A new generation has come to love and commit themselves to the ministry of CBCC. Today, most guests never knew Evangeline and Archie McNeill. Many have never met Heather Goodenough. Many are unfamiliar with the conference center's history. Though this new generation may not feel connected to that part of the conference center, they have experienced God's blessing here. And no matter what other changes may occur at Cannon Beach Christian Conference Center, He changes not.